The title is apt and the book is rich. The authors are both savvy apologists and leaders in the church. *Reasons to Believe* delivers solid answers in a winsome way, especially to those new to the vital discipline of Christian apologetics.

Douglas Groothuis
Ph.D., Professor of Philosophy, Denver Seminary

In my mind there's always enough room for another book that tackles the tough questions that challenge our faith. Unlike other similar books, editors Dennis Moles and Ryan Whitson have assembled a group of scholarly yet highly relevant responses to these age-old problems. Thanks to them for another great resource to bolster our faith!

Dr. Joseph M. Stowell
President, Cornerstone University, Grand Rapids, Mich.

Reasons to Believe is a well-researched work that covers the major problems people have with Christianity, and it does so in a winsome, easy-to-read style. Moles and Whitson have spent their lives around the local church, and they have learned to communicate to ordinary people in a language they can understand. I am happy to see this book be published and highly recommend it.

JP Moreland
Distinguished Professor of Philosophy, Biola University and author of *The Soul: How We Know It's Real and Why It Matters*.

At no time in modern history have Christian beliefs and values experienced such a deluge of criticism, questions, and attacks as they are today. As our Western culture drifts further from its Judeo-Christian moorings, believers are often left feeling at best marginalized, and at other times accosted by diverse worldviews and cultural values. *Reasons to Believe* is a great resource in Christian apologetics for the ordinary believer. The compilation of articles cover many of the questions which believers and non-believers struggle with for understanding and answers. The various authors do a good job of explaining unfamiliar terms and supporting their articles from diverse sources. Most importantly they bring practical application of a Christian worldview to some of the most pressing issues so foundational to understanding life.

Stan Rieb
Executive Director, Rocky Mountain Church Network and National Facilitator for CBAmerica

It's one thing to have belief, but another to have conviction, as conviction comes from testing a belief and finding it to be true. *Reasons to Believe* is a fine dialogue partner along this journey, exploring the biggest challenges to Christian faith in one handy title. Don't just read this book—ponder it, question it, put its ideas to the test. By doing so, I think you'll find yourself with some new convictions.

Sheridan Voysey
Writer, speaker, broadcaster, and author of *Resilient*,
Resurrection Year*, and *Unseen Footprints: Encountering the
Divine Along the Journey of Life.

Dennis Moles and Ryan Whitson have given a valuable gift to the Church by providing easy access to the answers to critical questions about the faith. This book reads naturally as though one is in a comfortable conversation with a close and wise friend. Although the answers are tested over time and orthodox to the core, they are presented with an irenic spirit and familiar vocabulary. *Reasons to Believe* is a must read for anyone who has struggled with questions about their faith or wants to speak clearly with those who do.

Chris Miller
Senior Professor of Biblical Studies, Cedarville University

As a follower of Christ, we are to "Always be prepared to give an answer for the hope that you have" (I Peter 3:15). In *Reasons to Believe*, editors Dennis Moles and Ryan Whitson, with the help of several contributing authors, have given the church a gift to help equip us with those answers. They do not shy away from the difficult questions, and they use solid scholarship and practical wisdom to help address those questions. I am delighted to recommend it to anyone who wants "to give a reason for the hope" they have.

Bill Higley
Ph.D., Vice President of Academics at Summit University,
Clarks Summit, Pennsylvania

— Moral principle is the same as Ethics
— Ethics are principles that are accepted
as right and wrong in a group or
society.

REASONS
TO
BELIEVE

Morality is what is wrong. or
is wrong or deals with right
& wrong.

REASONS
TO
BELIEVE

Thoughtful Responses
to Life's
Tough Questions

Dennis B. Moles
Ryan P. Whitson

Reasons to Believe – Dennis B. Moles & Ryan P. Whitson
Copyright © 2016
First edition published 2016

Editors: Jeremiah Zeiset, Sheila Wilkinson, and Ruth Zetek

Printed in the United States of America
Aneko Press – *Our Readers Matter*™
www.anekopress.com
Aneko Press, Life Sentence Publishing, and our logos are trademarks of
Life Sentence Publishing, Inc.
203 E. Birch Street
P.O. Box 652
Abbotsford, WI 54405
RELIGION / Christian Life / Spiritual Growth
Paperback ISBN: 978-1-62245-306-1
eBook ISBN: 978-1-62245-307-8
10 9 8 7 6 5 4 3 2 1
Available where books are sold
Share this book on Facebook:

Contents

Introduction

'm a believer – a Christian. I (Dennis) was born into a Christian home with Christian parents. My dad pastored several churches while I was growing up; my grandfather served his local church as a deacon for over fifty years; and my great-grandfather, so they tell me, sang bass in a gospel quartet. I have been involved in some form of vocational Christian ministry all of my adult life. I'm a "lifer" and an insider.

I also have had many questions about what I was taught in the church and what I believe as a follower of Christ. I remember lying in bed as a teenager wondering to myself, "How do I *know* that God exists?" As I got older, the questions became more troubling. "Can I be sure that Christianity is *right* and other religions are wrong? How can there be an all-loving and all-powerful God when there is so much evil in the world? Can I really trust that the Bible is true?"

For many years, I wrestled in silence with my doubts and questions. I attempted to persist in my belief and tried not to think about my questions. Occasionally I would feel safe enough to share my misgivings with someone and usually found the honest sharing helpful. During these times of transparency, I learned two key truths that reinforce the need for books like this one:

1. Almost everyone has questions or doubts.

2. There are good, solid reasons to believe in the Christian faith.

Why One More Book?

Why one more book on reasons for the Christian faith? Because people still struggle with faith questions and need solid, logical answers to their questions. *Reasons to Believe* is built on the premise that men and women still need answers to their legitimate faith questions. You or someone you know may have pressing questions or gentle curiosities regarding God, the Bible, and some of the topics addressed in this book. Wherever you are in your spiritual journey, we wrote this book as a resource that helps you see that the Christian faith is reasonable and trustworthy.

In recent years, New Atheists like Sam Harris, Richard Dawkins, and the late Christopher Hitchens have written extensively and debated vigorously on behalf of their worldview.[1] As a result, they have exerted an influence on society that has created a climate of doubt among believers, especially younger Christians. Many believers are facing arguments that they are not equipped to handle, and their appeals to biblical authority are met with mockery and scorn. What is needed are tools for dealing with contemporary attacks on Christianity in order to reassure believers of the truth of biblical faith and teach them how to meet attacks on biblical Christianity head-on with effective and thoughtful responses.

Who Will Benefit from This Book?

Reasons to Believe was written to be understandable, accessible, and useful for anyone who wants to know more about the Christian faith. This book addresses ten questions we consider the most pressing topics for the church today. These are

1   **Worldview**: A philosophical way of looking at life and how the world works.

the questions we find people in the church wrestling with the most and the same questions that often keep the unchurched away from considering the claims of the Bible for themselves. In this way, we believe this book has value for you regardless of where you are in your spiritual journey.

Several years ago, before I graduated from seminary, I had a wonderful phone conversation with my eighty-year-old grandfather. He had called to congratulate me on my upcoming graduation. He asked about the kids; I asked if he had been fishing; he talked about getting the old boat fixed and back in the river; and then the conversation took an unexpected turn. "Son [my grandfather calls me *Son*], since you're graduating from seminary, I need to ask you a question." He paused. "You can read Greek, can't you? I mean, can you read the Bible the way it was originally written down?"

I was a bit puzzled by his question but told him that with a little help from my lexicon, I could decipher the Greek text competently.

"I've been wondering for all of my life and never knew anyone to ask ... Son, can I trust my Bible? I mean, is my Bible, the one I read in English, the same as the original Bible?"

My grandfather is one of the godliest men I have ever known, but just because someone is godly does not mean they have answers to all their questions. That afternoon I talked with him about how the books of the Bible were selected. I told him about translation practices, archeological evidence, and the unbelievable consistency in ancient biblical manuscripts. The more I talked, the more amazed he became. When we hung up the phone that day, I realized that I had given away something very precious, but in the process of giving, I had lost nothing. That night my grandfather read his Bible with a renewed and informed confidence.

How to Read This Book

Reasons to Believe is a compilation of ten essays on different topics authored by different writers. Each chapter speaks to one important question and, as a result, does not necessarily build on the previous chapter. Therefore, you are free to read this book front to back or jump around by picking the chapters that most interest you.

Also, included with each chapter are discussion questions. It is our way of encouraging you to think through these questions and write down your thoughts to help process the material. If possible, we would encourage you to gather a group to read this book together and use the questions to start a conversation. Talking through your convictions and questions and listening to others is a valuable learning tool that will help you immensely.

Please think of *Reasons to Believe* as more like a walking stick to accompany you on your spiritual journey and not a club to be used on those who do not agree with your worldview. Read these pages with humility, a hunger to learn, and a desire to both grow in your relationship with God and help others discover the truth.

When reading this book, please keep two very important things in mind. First, none of us can argue someone else into a relationship with God. Remember the Holy Spirit's role. He convicts, He draws, He regenerates, He saves, and He seals our salvation; rely on Him to accomplish His will. Second, our job is to faithfully tell others the good news of Jesus Christ. Books like *Reasons to Believe* give us tools for telling others about Jesus. They don't guarantee a particular result, because every conversation and every relationship is different and unique. If we understand our role (to faithfully, clearly, and passionately witness) in light of God's role (to seek and to save the lost), we will experience joy and freedom in our conversations. True joy is found when we let God do His job and we do ours.

As a final word of encouragement, don't forget to pray as you read. Ask God to show you what He wants you to learn, know, process, and consider. Pray for those you will have conversations with. Pray for a gentle and respectful spirit in your interactions. Pray, because God forbid we win an argument but lose an opportunity to show the persistent and pursuing love of Christ. And as you enter into meaningful and redemptive conversations, know that we – the authors and editors – are praying for you.

Chapter 1

Can We Know What We Believe?

By Danny Loe

Ben revved the engine and climbed out of his car. "Thanks again for the jump, Jared," he said, disconnecting the cables. "I guess it's time to break down and invest in a new battery."

"No problem," his neighbor replied. "You can call me anytime."

Ben took a deep breath and plunged in, "By the way, Bev and I have been meaning to invite you and Marcia to a concert that our church is sponsoring next Friday. It's supposed to be a pretty good band."

"Church?" Jared repeated, hissing air in through his teeth as he shook his head. "Sorry, but I'm really not into religious stuff. I think it's great that you guys believe the way you do, but I'm more of a facts kind of person." He grinned. "Hey, I'm an engineer, what else would you expect?"

Ben shrugged nonchalantly. "Well, okay, but let me know if you change your mind." As Jared backed his car out of the driveway, Ben frowned and said to himself, "I really wanted to say more, but that comment of his got under my skin. What did he mean, saying that he's a 'facts kind of person'? Does my believing the Bible mean I'm not?"

Mark Twain, the great American author of the nineteenth

and early-twentieth centuries, once wrote, "Faith is believing what you know ain't so."[1] Though the words were written to be humorous, this understanding of faith actually describes what many skeptics[2] believe: Faith is unrelated to the concepts of reason, evidence, and knowledge.[3] Unfortunately, this misunderstanding is not limited to agnostics[4] and atheists. Many Christians also accept a more subtle version of Twain's description of faith.

Media bombardment of Christians with this perspective does not help. Some in the media tell followers of Jesus that religion in general, and Christianity in particular, is at best an emotional security blanket, or at worst, a source of evil in the world. Bill Maher, a popular comedian, television host, and political commentator, offered these strong words on the topic of faith:

> The irony of religion is that because of its power to divert man to destructive courses, the world could actually come to an end. The plain fact is, religion must die for mankind to live. The hour is getting very late to be able to indulge in having key decisions made by religious people. . . . Faith means making a virtue out of not thinking. It's nothing to brag about. And those who preach faith, and enable and elevate it are intellectual

---

1   Mark Twain (Samuel Clemens), "The Project Gutenberg EBook of The Entire Project Gutenberg Works of Mark Twain," *www.gutenberg.org/dirs/3/2/0/3200/3200.txt* (December 15, 2012).

2   **Skepticism**: Doubt as to the truth of something; the theory that certain knowledge is impossible.

3   J. P. Moreland and Klaus Issler, *In Search of a Confident Faith* (Downers Grove, IL: InterVarsity Press, 2008), 17-18. Here is a quote by an atheist: "It might sound a bit harsh or extreme to say that religious faith entails believing and asserting as true ideas a person knows perfectly well are false, but sometimes this conclusion is inescapable." Austin Cline, Comment of the Week: Faith is Believing What You Know Ain't So, *atheism.about.com/b/2010/01/19 comment-of-the-week-faith-is-believing-what-you-know-aint-so.htm* (December 15, 2012).

4   **Agnosticism**: The idea that it is impossible for a person to attain knowledge of a certain subject matter, especially in regards to God.

slaveholders, keeping mankind in a bondage to fantasy and nonsense that has spawned and justi-fied so much lunacy and destruction. Religion is dangerous because it allows human beings who don't have all the answers to think that they do.[1]

This kind of verbal abuse of faith and religion is not limited to comedians. Highly esteemed physicist Stephen Hawking, speaking to the U.K.'s *The Guardian* newspaper, said, "I regard the brain as a computer which will stop working when its com-ponents fail. There is no heaven or afterlife for broken-down computers; that is a fairy story for people afraid of the dark."[2]

With this kind of opposition to belief in God being promoted in such reasonable-sounding tones by society's heroes of literature, entertainment, and science, it is no wonder believers are tempted to feel like second-class thinkers who may well have deceived themselves. Oxford academic Richard Dawkins said in an interview posted in the Washington Post, "… but the arrogance of a religious person who just *knows* – not only knows that there's a god but knows it's *this* God, it's the Christian God, it's the trinity, and the Virgin Mary was born of a virgin. I mean they've got it all written down pat, and they've got absolutely not a shred of evidence for any of it. *That's* arrogance."[3] Dawkins is not content merely to disagree personally with the possibility of a reasonable knowledge about God, but he is aggressively taking

> *This kind of verbal abuse of faith and religion is not limited to comedians.*

---

1   IMDb, "Religulous," *www.imdb.com/title/tt0815241/quotes* (December 15, 2012). There are many alarming statements in this quote as well as other kinds of errone-ous reasoning, but it is indicative of some of the more virulent opposition faced by believers today.

2   Ian Sample, "Stephen Hawking: 'There is no heaven; it's a fairy story,'" The Guardian, May 15, 2011, *www.guardian.co.uk/science/2011/may/15/stephen-hawking-interview-there-is-no-heaven* (December 15, 2012).

3   Sally Quinn, "Divine Impulses: Richard Dawkins on 'the arrogance of religious per-sons'" (online video), Washington Post, *www.washingtonpost.com/wp-dyn/content/video/2009/11/30/VI2009113003185.html?hpid= talkbox1* (December 15, 2012).

the battle to people of faith. Speaking at the Reason Rally in Washington, D.C., he called on his audience to "mock them, ridicule them."[1]

Christian philosopher Dallas Willard was probably right when he wrote that many believers fear deep inside that "something has been found out that renders a spiritual understanding of reality in the matter of Jesus simply foolish to those who are 'in the know.'"[2] Closer examination reveals that these people "in the know" rarely offer any solid evidence for their negative assertions about religion. Rather, they merely repeat that faith is not reasonable and that Christians can't actually know the truth they claim to believe, because there is nothing there to know. The authoritative air of those who mock Christianity rises from their underlying assumption that faith is nothing more than a personal preference. In order to understand if our belief is reasonable, and if it is based upon a genuine knowledge of reality, we need to look at both the nature of faith and the nature of knowledge.

What Is Faith?

Was Mark Twain correct? Is faith really believing something that we know is not so? Is it merely wishful thinking? The prevalent misconception about faith is that it is a "blind" trust, divorced from the kind of thinking that an educated, intelligent person would practice. The mindset that faith and reason are incompatible assumes that when considering spiritual and moral claims, faith is needed because there is no real knowledge of or

---

1   Kandis Smith, "Richard Dawkins' Reason Rally speech!" (YouTube video) https://youtu.be/RkyAE724d0k(December 3, 2012). This line received tremendous applause. Dawkins' purpose in this speech (at least in part) was to call atheists to put aside politeness and take their argument confidently to believers. Although, he later claimed in an interview with National Public Radio that he was referring not to believers, but to their beliefs. In either case, our point is made. The Reason Rally was an event celebrating secularism and atheism, held in Washington, D.C., on March 24, 2012. About 20,000 attended.

2   Dallas Willard, *The Divine Conspiracy* (New York: HarperCollins Publishers, 1998), 92.

evidence for the truth of those kinds of claims, but faith is not needed when considering scientific or other "objective" facts.[1] The truth is that every person who claims to know anything at all exercises a certain level of faith. People usually believe (have faith) in only those things for which there is an abundance of evidence.[2] Most people find it very difficult to believe something that obviously is not true, in spite of what Twain or Dawkins may have claimed. For instance, in a court case, the members of a jury hear the relevant evidence and draw a conclusion about the facts of the case. They don't make their decision based upon how they feel or whether they personally like the defendant (at least they shouldn't!).[3] Instead, their belief in the defendant's guilt or innocence is based upon knowledge of the facts or evidence. God created people with a mind that has the ability to evaluate evidence, to reason, and to believe.[4]

Since the word *faith* is so often used to refer to a belief that is irrational, it may help to think of faith as confidence. This will enable a person to understand faith more accurately as "trusting what we have reason to believe."[5] Properly understood, confidence (faith) is shown to be reliable by the nature of the evidence and knowledge that we have.

A reasonable confidence, or faith, has three elements. First, there is the content of a belief or what the belief is about (for example, I believe eating apples is good for my health). Second, there is a person's level of agreement with the content. Regarding eating apples, I can point to several reasons or evidences to support my belief that apples should be part of a healthy diet.

1   Moreland and Issler, *In Search of a Confident Faith*, 16.
2   Ibid., 18.
3   Garrett J. DeWeese and J. P. Moreland, *Philosophy Made Slightly Less Difficult: A Beginner's Guide to Life's Big Questions* (Downers Grove, IL: InterVarsity Press, 2005), 53.
4   Ibid.
5   Ibid.

This third aspect of faith is personal; it is a person's commitment to what they believe (for example, I will choose to eat a few apples each week). But notice that this third aspect is based on the first two elements of faith. The key is that knowledge comes first and is followed by a thoughtful acceptance. As an example, Romans 10:14 mirrors this progression when it says that man needs first to hear (content), then believe (acceptance of that content), and then call on the Lord (commitment).[1]

It is possible to have an intellectual understanding of the facts of the Christian faith but still struggle with agreement with those facts. This is demonstrated by some who may understand the teachings of the Bible but willfully choose not to accept them as true. In other cases, people may struggle with doubt, which is an intellectual or emotional hindrance to belief. Thomas, one of Jesus' disciples, doubted for a time that Jesus was alive after His resurrection. He needed more evidence to believe than just the testimonies of the other disciples (John 20:24-25). Unfortunately, doubt can be misunderstood by other Christians as unbelief or a sign of spiritual immaturity, when what is needed is a safe place to ask honest questions and receive helpful evidence for belief. This reality is a discipleship opportunity for the church to dialog and coach one another toward confident biblical faith that results in spiritual maturity.[2]

We also need to recognize that faith comes in degrees. This means a person will likely hold some beliefs with certainty, while they may be more unsure of other beliefs. In the latter case, they may be easily convinced to change their mind. In this way, these beliefs are usually not an all-or-nothing proposition.[3] It should be the goal of all Christians to strengthen their beliefs,

---

1   Ibid., 18-21.
2   It is certainly the goal of this book to be a resource for the church to help build confident biblical faith resulting in spiritual maturity. As each chapter tackles an important question, it is our hope that helpful reasons to believe will be provided.
3   DeWeese and Moreland, *Philosophy Made Slightly Less Difficult*, 21, 24.

but in this effort, it is essential to remember that confidence depends upon the object of faith and its trustworthiness. As an example, if I place my faith in something that is not true (that is, it doesn't correspond to reality), then unfortunate consequences will result. God wants people to believe in what is true and what will lead a person to become spiritually healthy. Therefore, the goal is always to hold true beliefs.

What Is Truth?

Faith, or confidence, is only as valid as its object; it depends upon truth. Since no one wants to believe in what is false, our goal should always be to seek out and believe whatever is true. Yet seeking the truth raises an important question: What exactly *is* truth?

Something is true if it corresponds to reality, if it lines up with the way things really are.[1] For example, if I say, "John is reading a book," that statement is only true if it aligns with reality and John is reading. But if John is playing a video game, then we would say the statement is not true. Therefore, the truth of a statement does not depend upon the person who says it or the level of sincerity with which it is made, but it depends on whether or not it corresponds to reality. In this way, it is nonsense to say that the claim "John is reading a book" is true for you but not for me, since all we need to do is measure the claim to the reality of John's actions.

Faith, or confidence, is only as valid as its object; it depends upon truth.

Unfortunately, it is common today to hear statements such as "Your religious beliefs are true for you but not for me." This

---

1   Kenneth Richard Samples, *A World of Difference: Putting Christian Truth-Claims to the Worldview Test* (Grand Rapids, MI: Baker Books, 2007), Kindle Electronic Edition: Location 74. Dawkins and Twain are right if the meaning of faith that we infer from their writings is correct. But I hope that by this time we have made it clear that they hold that faith is unrelated to reality. This is not the faith that Christians, or the Bible, hold to be genuine.

too is nonsensical, since truth is determined by how it lines up with reality, not by the one who believes it. Either the religious belief is true or it is not. The fact that I believe, even fervently, that something is true does not make it true. Therefore, faith is to depend on the reliability of the *object* of the belief. In other words, truth is always *objective*.

What about subjective truth, where the person making the claim would be the determiner of truth? This does not actually exist in real life. No one has the ability to instantaneously change reality by his claims. For example, the phrase "I believe John is Irish" is an example of personal belief, but not of subjective truth. If John is in actuality Dutch, my belief cannot determine or change the truth of his nationality, no matter how strongly I hold the belief that he is Irish. Some people think that subjective truth exists, because they confuse the concept with subjective preference. They may protest – "Isn't it the case that some truths *are* subjective, such as the statement 'I prefer coffee to tea'? Not everyone prefers coffee to tea, so this must be a subjective truth, right?" No. The reason for this is that my claim still corresponds to reality – it is true that I do indeed prefer coffee. It's easy to speak as if subjective truth actually exists because we humans tend to state our personal beliefs as propositions of truth. Who hasn't made statements like "My mother makes the best chocolate cake in the world" or "Mac is better than PC"? However, being firmly convinced that your beliefs are true, even though others may disagree, does not make them subjective truth.

The important concept to grasp is that for something to be true, it must correspond to reality. It can be easy for a Christian to believe that spiritual or biblical truth is somehow different or inferior to truth in the secular realm.[1] A Jesus-follower must

---

1   Nancy Pearcey, *Total Truth: Liberating Christianity from Its Cultural Captivity* (Wheaton, IL: Crossway Books, 2004), 22-24. Pearcey has a helpful discussion on the "heart and brain" two-level view of truth that has been accepted by many believers.

understand and be confident that they have as much right to objective truth-claims as the most esteemed scientists. The catch for both the nonbeliever and the Christian, whether evaluating a scientific hypothesis or a biblical doctrine, is that it is only valid and true if it corresponds to reality.

An important warning at this point is that, while people of all perspectives make truth-claims, not everyone handles the evidence perfectly or rationally. People may want to arrive at reasonable conclusions, but it is possible to be mistaken. A certain amount of humility is necessary, since we cannot know all that there is to know, nor can we always be sure that we have evaluated all the data properly. Therefore, it is important to carefully consider our assertions and thoughtfully gather our evidence to support our claims. Only when we have sufficient evidence of the right kind can we have greater confidence that what we believe is, in fact, true.

For example, mathematical truth-claims demand evidence of equations and numerical proofs, while scientific truth-claims may require experiments that are carried out time and time again to establish a pattern. Historical and philosophical truth-claims require yet other types of evidence. It would be pointless and intellectually dishonest to try to judge the reliability of a historical truth-claim in a chemistry laboratory.[1] Each different area of study requires its own appropriate kind of evidence,[2] although there may be some overlap at times. For example, the Christian faith is based on biblical evidence, but it may also draw on other areas, such as scientific evidence (for example, the design of a DNA molecule) or historical evidence (for example, the death and resurrection of Jesus Christ).

---

1   We recognize that sometime scientists may use chemical analysis on certain ancient materials, but this analysis is focused on a specific artifact. This may contribute to the acceptance of a historical truth-claim, but this does not negate our point that the general flow of historical events is not a matter for chemistry to test.

2   DeWeese and Moreland, *Philosophy Made Slightly Less Difficult*, 69; David A. Horner, *Mind Your Faith* (Downers Grove, IL: InterVarsity Press, 2011), 74-75.

In conclusion, how can Christians have confidence that they can handle the evidence for their faith in a valid, rational way? They can have confidence that the claims of the Bible are objectively true in that they correspond to reality. In addition, Christians can have confidence that the Holy Spirit uses their minds and ability to think critically about various topics and can guide them in understanding and accepting truths that might otherwise be missed.[1] The key is understanding that faith is not divorced from reason nor is it divorced from genuine knowledge of truth. It is a confidence which comes not from feelings and desires, but from knowledge about reality. Therefore, a person can say with confidence that Mark Twain was wrong. It is possible to know that a belief is true.

It is possible to know that a belief is true.

What Is Knowledge?

If faith depends on reason and knowledge, then it is important to understand knowledge. Knowledge can be defined as "either an accurate experiential awareness of reality or a true belief about reality based on adequate grounds."[2] When it comes to daily life, we all want people around us who are knowledgeable. For example, if my computer stops working, I want to be able to call someone who knows about computers and can fix my problem. I would not ask a toddler to fix my computer, because he would not have knowledge in this area.[3] The key is that we live our daily lives under the assumption that knowledge is real

---

1   Horner, *Mind Your Faith*, 75-76.
2   Moreland and Issler, *In Search of a Confident Faith*, 41.
3   Just as it is not wise to go to an auto mechanic for help in repairing my computer, it does not seem wise to go to an atheist to help me understand faith in God. A quick look at atheist websites, or reader comments on articles found on similar websites, reveals that these people often have little knowledge or understanding of the assertions they make about Scripture, Christianity, etc. It's unfortunate to see blogs where people seek input on the existence or character of God from authorities in other areas who have no knowledge of God's Word or spiritual matters.

and useful. Similarly, we need to recognize that we are able to know things when it comes to matters of faith.

From a biblical perspective, knowledge is not only possible but also expected.[1] Luke states his reason for writing his gospel account, *so that you may know the exact truth about the things you have been taught* (Luke 1:4 NASB). Jesus said in John 8:32, *and you will know the truth and the truth will set you free.* Look carefully at what Jesus and Luke both assumed when they made these statements. They were assuming that it is possible for a person to have genuine, life-changing knowledge of the truth. Faith is to be grounded in knowledge and truth.

We can recognize three types of knowledge, each of which is gained in different ways. First, there is personal knowledge, which is also called knowledge by acquaintance. This knowledge comes from knowing a person or a thing directly.[2] For example, if I received a new bicycle for my birthday, I would know my new bike first by looking it over or getting acquainted with its features. This kind of knowledge includes not only what we can experience with our five senses (for example, looking over the new bicycle or touching the handlebars), but also things like our own personal thoughts, feelings, desires, memories, and even God Himself and the Spirit's guidance.[3] All people, Christian or not, have this kind of knowledge. But an important distinction Christians enjoy is not only knowing about Jesus Christ intellectually but also knowing Him personally. In this way, a Christian can have personal knowledge of the Son of God.

The next type of knowledge is called know-how or skill knowledge. We acquire this knowledge when we actually learn how to do something. Going back to my previous example, I

---

1   Samples, *A World of Difference*, 76.

2   DeWeese and Moreland, *Philosophy Made Slightly Less Difficult*, 54-55; Horner, *Mind Your Faith*, 80.

3   J. P. Moreland, *Kingdom Triangle: Recover the Christian Mind, Renovate the Soul, Restore the Spirit's Power* (Grand Rapids, MI: Zondervan, 2007), 127.

gained this type of knowledge when I learned how to ride my new bicycle or take care of it. I gained this knowledge when I learned a new skill. As another example, I learned to fly an airplane as a young man, so I can say that I have a certain level of "know-how" when it comes to taking off, landing, and other skills related to flying. Christians need know-how knowledge in order to live as God has commanded, whether knowing how to read and study the Bible, pray, or minister to other people.

These two types of knowledge – personal and know-how – depend upon the third type of knowledge – propositional. Propositional knowledge is knowing facts. The famous Greek philosopher Plato came up with the understanding that propositional knowledge is the same as justified true belief (that is, it is legitimate, it is true, and you believe it). Although this understanding has been challenged over time, it is still the standard, clearest description available for propositional knowledge. Plato's view of knowledge says that there are three conditions that lead to knowledge that a proposition (statement) is true.[1]

Condition #1: Belief

A person must first believe something is true before they can confidently say that they *know* it's true. For example, my money is deposited safely in a bank and insured by the government. However, if I don't believe that my money is truly safe, the most I can say is, "I hope my money is safe." I can't confidently boast, "I know my money is safe," unless I actually believe that it is. Of course, believing something (that is, my money is safe) doesn't *make* it true, but I won't acknowledge that I know something unless I also believe it.[2] Even though skeptics may say things like, "I don't need faith; I have scientific knowledge," the fact is that they cannot have knowledge, even scientific knowledge,

---

1   Horner, *Mind Your Faith*, 76.
2   DeWeese and Moreland, *Philosophy Made Slightly Less Difficult*, 56; Horner, *Mind Your Faith*, 76.

without belief. In reality, they only say they know certain things *because* they believe them![1] Of course, belief can't be the only condition for knowledge, because it is possible to believe things that are not true. This leads to the next condition for knowledge.

Condition #2: Truth

It is the nature of people to want to believe things that are true. In addition, a person can only know something that is true. If I say I *know* the moon is made of blue cheese, I may have all the confidence in the world that my assertion is true and that I have knowledge about this, but because the moon is not made of blue cheese (according to reality), my belief is not knowledge. In other words, I cannot know the moon is made of blue cheese, because it is not. However, under the right circumstances, it is possible to believe something that is true without having knowledge of it. For instance, suppose my watch says that it's 3:30, but unknown to me, my watch is broken and simply stuck on this time. When asked by others, I gladly share that the time is 3:30, but my reply, at best, would only be true twice every twenty-four hours. Now, imagine I was asked for the time at exactly 3:30, and I was able to report the time accurately. In this situation, even though I gave a truthful answer, I did not have real knowledge that it was 3:30. This shows that even though truth is necessary for knowledge, it is not sufficient by itself to enable a person to say that they have knowledge. To have real knowledge and the confidence that it provides, they must also have justification for their true beliefs.

Condition #3: Justification

Finally, a person should have reasons to believe (justification) what they know is true. If we want to have knowledge based on justified true beliefs, then we must believe the right kinds of

---

1   Horner, *Mind Your Faith*, 67, 73.

things for the right kinds of reasons. When Christians ground their beliefs on how sincerely they feel or on a cultural expectation that something must be true or acceptable, they are not basing their beliefs on a solid foundation.[1] After all, it is possible to feel a deep sense of certainty about something and yet be completely wrong. Therefore, we should be justified in holding the beliefs that we do. Naturally, this raises the question: What are sufficient grounds for accepting something as truth? How much and what kind of evidence do we need for our beliefs to be rationally justified? Is absolute certainty required? To help us answer these questions, we need to look at two ways that people tend to justify their beliefs. These two ways are called coherentism and foundationalism.[2]

First, coherentism holds that "a belief is justified if and only if it is coherent (or consistent) with a person's other justified beliefs."[3] According to this theory, our beliefs are validated by our other beliefs. This perspective is based on the idea that a certain logical consistency exists within a group of beliefs. But is this good enough evidence to justify each individual belief as true? No, it is not. It is very possible to build a belief structure that is coherent, but that does not correspond to reality. For example, the *Star Wars* movie series has created a large web of coherent beliefs about the Jedi, the Dark Side, and the Force. But while these movies present a coherent set of ideas, they don't necessarily correspond to reality such that they are actually true. Those who accept the theory of coherentism as a way to justify their beliefs have decided there is no way to know if any individual beliefs are actually true in reality and if those beliefs are therefore reliable enough to base

> ...we must believe the right kinds of things for the right kinds of reasons.

---

1   Moreland and Issler, *In Search of a Confident Faith*, 47.
2   DeWeese and Moreland, *Philosophy Made Slightly Less Difficult*, 62.
3   Ibid., 64-66.

their other beliefs upon. While it is important that our beliefs are consistent so we do not contradict ourselves, coherentism cannot provide a foundation for our knowledge of the world as it is. As Christians, we must reject this approach to justifying what we believe.

On the other hand, foundationalism says that a "belief is justified if and only if it is properly basic or is based on properly basic beliefs."[1] This means that something is only worth believing if it is not based on what you or other people think, but rather is built on something so basic that everyone just knows that it is true. A classic example of foundational knowledge would be that all rational people just "know" that it is wrong to torture babies for fun. Of course, you will then ask, "What else does everyone 'just know' to be true?" There are two ideas of how to understand this "you-just-know-it" foundational knowledge. The first idea is called classical foundationalism and the second is called modest foundationalism.

Classical foundationalism says that a belief is only justified if it has grounds that guarantee its truth. This means a person can only know something that cannot possibly be doubted, which severely limits what a person can know. Therefore, without access to much knowledge that is beyond any doubt, the classical foundationalist model fails. This has led some people over the centuries to throw out foundationalism altogether and turn to coherentism or, more recently, to postmodernism and the idea that absolute truth does not exist.[2] Thankfully, another option to explore is modest foundationalism.

Modest foundationalism says that a person is justified in believing something even though it is possible to question it. However, modest foundationalism does require that a statement be reasonable and conducive to the truth before it can be

---

1   Ibid., 63.
2   Moreland and Issler, *In Search of a Confident Faith*, 47-48.

accepted. In other words, the evidence that a person bases their belief on must show that it is *probable* that the belief is true. For example, you can justify beliefs that cannot rationally be doubted. One doesn't doubt things that are self-evident (2 + 2 = 4), things that can't be challenged (I am a thinking being that exists), or things that are evident to the senses (I'm experiencing a feeling of cold).[1] Some form of this modest foundationalism is the most reasonable approach we finite humans have in justifying our beliefs.

Two Contemporary Challenges to Christians

Christians need to be careful not to buy into two dangerous assumptions prevalent in our society today. The first is the naturalist's claim that nothing exists beyond the natural universe and its laws of nature, and that one cannot know truth except through empirical evidence. Many people think that scientific proof equals absolute proof. It is certainly presented that way in our media and in the classroom. The truth is that there is more data and more to know about the physical world than finite scientists will ever be able to exhaust. In light of this seemingly unlimited data, even the best scientific conclusions may be based on partial and incomplete evidence. This does not mean that all scientific conclusions are wrong, but it does mean that the scientist's claim to certainty is not as justified as society often insists that it is. In addition, many kinds of truth cannot be justified by scientific data. For example, mathematical, historical, and psychological truths cannot be scientifically proven. In addition, not all assertions from scientists are based on scientific knowledge, such as when Stephen Hawking made his claim that there is no God and no heaven. In this case, he is making a philosophical and theological assertion, *not* a scientific statement. Unfortunately, many people assume his

1   Ibid., 68.

statements reflect scientific knowledge rather than personal opinion because of his status as a scientist. Philosophical and theological statements about meaning, morality, and the spiritual realm cannot accurately be evaluated scientifically. Scientific proof is neither absolute nor sufficient to confer justification on all areas of knowledge.

Conclusion

As a Christian, you are not doomed to be at the mercy of those who aggressively push an atheistic agenda, claiming to have knowledge that cannot be refuted. The truth is that atheists have the same need to justify their beliefs as anyone else. They have not cornered the market on absolute certainty no matter what they claim. Christians have good, sound reasons for believing and knowing the truth about what the Bible teaches about God, mankind, and salvation. A Christian does have rational justification to hold these beliefs, as well as many other propositions about spiritual and moral matters. This should infuse the Christian with confidence that refuses to allow them to be intellectually bullied by other worldviews. This should also motivate the follower of Jesus to study the Bible and all other available evidence that justifies God-honoring beliefs. The chapters that follow will present evidence on a variety of topics that help justify that you can know what you believe is true.

> *The truth is that atheists have the same need to justify their beliefs as anyone else.*

---

1   Horner, *Mind Your Faith*, 81.

Discussion Questions

- How has your definition of faith been impacted as a result of this chapter?

- Has there been a time in your life when you felt intimidated by others because of what you believe? What happened? How did you handle it?

- Truth is what corresponds to reality. Why is this definition of truth so important?

Chapter 2

Is It Reasonable to Believe in God?

By Darrell Dooyema

W hat really makes you tick?"
I shifted nervously in my chair, realizing I was not prepared for this question during a job interview. How should I answer? Should I profess my belief in God, my hope in Jesus Christ as the salvation of my soul, my hope for eternity, and my purpose in life given by Him? Would I risk being thought strange, perhaps not getting the job as a result of my "religious" answer? Yet how could I be an honest believer and not answer this question? What else could I say "really makes me tick"? I resolved to share my faith with my potential future employer and proceeded to explain God's love for us, our problem with sin, God's solution to this problem, and my hope for eternity. When I had finished, the interviewer paused for a moment and reflected, "Hmmm ... that is very interesting for you. Want to know what really makes me tick? I ride motorcycles."

I was astonished! He compared ultimate purpose in life to a weekend hobby. His answer revealed that he thought the idea of God was a useful fantasy for some people, but not for him. He was content with his motorcycle.

Was he right? Is belief in God like riding motorcycles? Is it merely personal preference, perhaps a hobby for the incurably religious? Is it strange and unreasonable, something reserved for the superstitious or non-scientifically minded person? In this chapter, I will argue the opposite. In fact, belief in God is exceedingly reasonable, and the evidence for belief is overwhelming. We can know about God, and knowledge of God is of ultimate concern for all of us; indeed, it will affect us for all eternity.

Isn't it true that belief in God is all about faith? Why should a person worry about being reasonable if all that is needed is faith? Indeed, the Bible does call people to a position of faith and teaches that a person can't please God without faith.[1] Yet the Bible does not define faith as a blind, non-thinking leap. Instead, God invites us to use our reason, to dig deep, to figure things out, and to look for the best evidence. *"Come now, and let us reason together,"* God tells Isaiah.[2] Jesus reminds us to *"Love the Lord your God with all your heart and with all your soul and with all your mind."*[3] The apostles demonstrate this same perspective in their writings. Jude urges us to *contend for the faith.*[4] Peter tells his readers to *Always be prepared to give an answer to everyone who asks you to give the reason for the hope that you have. But do this with gentleness and respect.*[5] Paul could be found on an average day *arguing persuasively about the kingdom of God*[6] and *proving that Jesus is the Messiah.*[7] These biblical examples certainly do not portray

The Bible does not define faith as a blind, non-thinking leap.

1   Hebrews 11:1-6.
2   Isaiah 1:18 (NASB).
3   Matthew 22:37.
4   Jude 1:3.
5   1 Peter 3:15.
6   Acts 19:8.
7   Acts 9:22.

an unthinking or mindless faith. So why should we think that having faith means shutting off our minds?

Our culture has commandeered the word *faith* and redefined it to mean something that the Bible never meant. In our world, people often take faith to be some kind of blind optimism or groundless hope. This kind of faith is divorced from reason and even seems to fight against reason. This belief – that faith is a general positive feeling about life – is why many argue "it doesn't matter *what* you believe, just be sincere in your faith." But this hollow faith is not at all like the faith of the Bible.

Instead, the Bible teaches us that the *object* of faith is what validates it. In other words, faith is not valid based on its quality or quantity. Rather, faith is only valid if the thing you have faith in is trustworthy and true. Paul writes, *And if Christ has not been raised, our preaching is useless and so is your faith.*[1] If we have faith in something false, our faith is pointless – perhaps even dangerous.

For example, imagine that you are about to rappel off the side of a cliff and just before you step off the ledge, the instructor asks, "How strong is your faith in the rope?"

You answer, "It depends – how strong *is* the rope?"

You need faith in order to step off the cliff, but if the rope is weak, you will still fall to your death no matter how strong your faith is. If the instructor tells you, "It is about as strong as a piece of dental floss," you will most likely answer, "Find another volunteer!" The object of your faith, in this case the rope, must be strong in order for your faith to be valid.

The example above actually illustrates that biblical faith is the informed decision we make to step over the edge. We don't jump blindly off the cliff. Instead, we ask why we should believe that the rope is strong enough to hold us; then we step off the cliff in a state of trust. Similarly, God invites us to trust Him

---

1   1 Corinthians 15:14.

with our very lives, and He invites us to investigate the evidence
and understand the ideas that make trust in Him reasonable.
So, is belief in God reasonable? The only way to answer that
question is to look at the evidence and ask ourselves the question, "Is belief in God reasonable?"

The Cumulative Case

There are many arguments for the existence of God, and together
they make up what is often called the cumulative case. Each
individual argument in the cumulative case approaches the
question of God's existence a bit differently, and each argument has its strong points as well as its critics. Yet when we
stand back and consider all the arguments collectively, we see
clearly that the only rational conclusion is that God exists.
Philosophers call this process *abductive reasoning*. This is the
kind of reasoning crime-scene investigators use – the process
of deducing the truth regarding a situation by investigating
all the evidence and then offering the best explanation, given
what is known. Sherlock Holmes, as he snoops around making
deductions, employs this kind of reasoning as well. He examines
the facts and imagines what would best fit all that he sees. His
conclusions fit the evidence.

So what about the existence of God? We find evidence for
God all over the universe – in science, in logic, in nature, in
morality, in experience, and in history. In fact, this chapter
contains only a small stitch of the vast amount of evidence
that God has woven into the fabric of our world. As you think
through each of these arguments, consider how they contribute
to the larger case of our knowledge of God and His involve-
ment in our world.

A Common Objection to Cumulative Case Argumentation

Before we look at several pieces of evidence in favor of God's existence, we might want to anticipate one of the most common objections to cumulative case argumentation. Some will raise the objection that a chain is only as strong as its weakest link. They will argue that if any of the aspects in this cumulative case are not exceedingly strong, the whole case will fall apart. If they don't agree with (or even understand) one of the points of argument, then none of the other points are valid either. Yet this is a misunderstanding of what a cumulative case argument is. A cumulative case argument is not a chain of dependent links, but the gathering and investigation of evidence.

Instead of a chain, the cumulative case works like a rope. The strongest ropes are made up of thousands of strands of material. Though each small fiber has some strength itself, when woven together with all of the other strands, it becomes part of an exceedingly strong rope able to hold thousands of pounds.

Cumulative case arguments are often used in court. Imagine a case in which Smith is accused of stealing Jones's iPod. The prosecutor raises evidence one piece at a time. "Ladies and gentlemen, Smith is well known for coveting Jones's iPod."

At this point, the defense rises and yells out, "Objection! This is not enough to convict!"

The prosecutor then answers, "True, but there is more. Smith told Barnes yesterday that he planned to steal Jones's iPod."

Again, the defense attorney cries out, "Objection! This is not enough to convict!"

The prosecutor again agrees that this alone is not enough, yet continues on, "Moreover, Smith was present at the scene of the crime while the crime was being committed, as evidenced by these video monitors showing him entering and subsequently leaving the house."

Again, the defense rises to object, noting that the mere fact of Smith's presence by itself does not prove his guilt. Again and again, the prosecutor introduces evidence until the defense lawyer is finally silent, embarrassed by the huge amount of evidence to show the guilt of Smith. When the prosecutor gives his closing statement, he lists off the pile of evidence against Smith: "Smith is well known to have coveted Jones's iPod; Smith told others that he planned to steal it; Smith was present at the time of the iPod's disappearance; his fingerprints were at the crime scene; he bragged about the crime to his friends; and finally, he happens to be listening to the iPod right now!"

In this simple example, some of the evidence is weakly connected to the crime while other evidence is much stronger. The prosecutor weaves his rope by adding one fiber after another. When all of the evidence is considered together, the conclusion is clear. The same is true for the case for God's existence. Some arguments seem stronger than others. Yet, as we consider some evidences for God's existence as a cumulative case, we will see that the clearest and most reasonable conclusion is to admit that God exists.

Evidence from Design in the Universe: How Science Reveals the Fingerprints of God

Suppose you are out walking in the mountains and you strike your foot against something. You look down and discover a watch laying on the trail. You pick it up, look it over, and discover a beautiful watch that is still working and even has the correct time. You wonder how this watch could turn up on the trail in the mountains. Did someone drop it? Did it fall out of their bag? Never once do you imagine that the watch grew up all on its own, appearing by the process of chance or natural order. Never once do you assume that the watch evolved over time through undirected natural processes like wind and erosion. Rather, you recognize that the watch has been carefully designed and intended for the specific function of telling time. Someone had to construct it in just the right way with all of the numbers in the correct arrangement and the gears and gadgetry precisely tuned; otherwise, it would not perform its function. This intricate design, precise arrangement, and specific purpose tell us that a designer made the watch.[1]

The world and many of the things in it possess these same qualities of intricacy and design for specific purposes. Think of the human eye, the human brain, or DNA. Not only do these biological systems display complexity, but they also demonstrate specific purpose. If the parts of the eye were randomly assembled in another way, we would not be able to see. The most reasonable conclusion is that a grand designer planned for them to function.

The Bible makes the radical claim that we can look outside our window and see evidence for God. *The heavens declare the glory of God; the skies proclaim the work of his hands*, writes David in Psalm 19. All around us, the earth roars clues of God's creativity, power, and intricate design.

Some time ago, my friend toured London and thought he would have some fun with the locals. He clowned around, trying to get the serious palace guards to smile and the local bobbies to laugh. Standing under the famous clock tower, Big Ben, he asked a local policeman, "Hey, where is that big old clock – what's the name, Big Bertha or something?"

The local Londoner was not amused and answered curtly, "If you would just look up, you'd see it!"

According to the Bible, if we would just look up, look out, and look around, we would see that the whole world is full of evidence of God. By scientific investigation, we can observe that God has beautifully and precisely designed the world, a

---

1   This is a version of English philosopher William Paley's famous watchmaker analogy.

masterpiece of massive proportion. Paul writes, *For since the creation of the world God's invisible qualities—his eternal power and divine nature—have been clearly seen, being understood from what has been made, so that people are without excuse.*[1]

But what about evolution? Doesn't this theory prove that the watch illustration and the Bible are wrong? Many thought that Darwin's theory defeated the design argument by revealing a process (natural selection) that could produce change on its own. But this has not turned out to be the case. The design argument has gained new vigor in our time as modern science continues to discover the weaknesses of Darwin's theory and as technology develops new ways to observe our universe. The deeper we get, the more design elements we find. One tiny strand of human DNA, for example, contains vastly more actual information than any complex computer program on the planet! With powerful microscopes, we can peek in to the intricately complex structures and machines that operate within the cell, something that Darwin could never have imagined nor reconciled with his theory of slight modifications over time. In fact, Darwin himself anticipated that this could be a problem and wrote, "If it could be demonstrated that any complex organ existed which could not possibly have been formed by numerous successive slight modifications, my theory would absolutely break down."[2]

...modern science continues to discover the weaknesses of Darwin's theory...

Biologists continue to discover elements that cannot be explained by Darwin's theory. One example is the bacterial flagellum, a tail that operates like an outboard motor to propel the bacteria through liquid. This tiny structure contains over forty separate parts, which all need to be present and assembled

---

1   Romans 1:20.
2   Charles Darwin, *The Origin of Species*, Avenel 1st ed. (New York: Crown Publishers, 1979), 219.

in the correct order for the tail to work properly. If only one of the forty parts is missing, the tail would be a useless hindrance and get weeded out by natural selection. This small organelle defies explanation by the evolutionary model of slight, small, gradual change. Evolutionary theory cannot explain how all of these parts simultaneously appeared, assembled precisely, and worked together to perform an incredibly efficient function.

Astronomers and physicists have discovered the same fine-tuning on a cosmic scale as well. Numerous fundamental physical constants must be precisely tuned for life to exist. Some of these constants are the rate of the expansion of the universe, the strong nuclear force that holds protons and neutrons together, the electromagnetic force, and the force of gravity. If gravity, for example, were weaker or stronger by only a 1-in-10^{40} degree, stars like the sun would not exist and no planets could contain life. More than forty constants like this must be exactly arranged, or life as we know it would be impossible. It appears someone has tinkered with the numerous knobs that control the universe, arranging them precisely to allow for life.[1]

The most rational explanation for these fine-tuned, information-rich, purpose-filled, and beautiful aspects of our world is that they have been specifically designed by an intelligent being.

Evidence from First Causes:
What Got Everything Started?

Have you ever stopped to ask the questions: Where did the universe come from? Why is there something instead of nothing? What caused all of this? If you have, you have already begun to pursue what philosophers call the cosmological argument for God's existence. This is an argument about cause and effect. When you see an effect, like a scratch on the side of your car,

---

1   Robin Collins, "The Fine-Tuning Design Argument: A Scientific Argument for the Existence of God," *www.discovery.org/a/91.*

you immediately ask the question, "Who or what caused this?" This is a natural part of our human experience, since we recognize that effects have causes. Philosophers have even given this principle a name: The Principle of Sufficient Reason. Often abbreviated as PSR, the principle simply states, "For every effect, there must be a cause."

In high school biology class, I remember my teacher instructing us along these lines. "Nothing comes from nothing," she told us. "This is a law of science." What is more, she taught us to understand that things move from a state of order to a state of disorder. We also learned that, when left to themselves, things slow down rather than speed up. Chemical experiments don't create anything new; they just rearrange things into different products. The next week we began to learn about the origin of life and evolution. She taught us that in the beginning there was nothing; then Bang! There was something. That something began to arrange itself from simple proteins into complex living things. Confused by this contradiction, I raised my hand and said, "So you're saying that ultimately everything came from nothing?"

"Yes," she replied.

Again I queried, "Didn't we learn last week that nothing can come from nothing?"

"Yes," she replied.

"Doesn't this pose a problem?" I asked.

So how does the Principle of Sufficient Reason apply to the question of God's existence? When we look at the enormous amount of effects around us in the universe, we naturally want to look for causes. This is part of what makes science fun. Yet each time we find a cause, we discover there is another cause that comes before. For example, when we discover that gravity caused my ice cream cone to fall to the ground, we have a new set of questions. What caused gravity? When a science teacher instructs us that gravity is caused by attraction of large cosmic bodies (like planets), we have more questions. What caused the planets? On and on we go until we realize there needs to be something solid at the beginning of all these causes. We need a *first cause* and this first cause needs to be solid enough to need no other explanation.

Why does this cause need to be so solid? Why can't we just think there are an infinite number of causes that go back and back without an end?[1] To answer these questions, imagine that you wanted to borrow a bicycle from your friend Marty, so you ask him for it. Marty replies, "I don't have one, but I'll ask Gloria."

Yet when Marty asks Gloria, she replies, "I don't have one either, but I'll ask Alex."

Alex then answers, "I don't have one either, but I'll ask Melman."

Melman keeps up the game and answers, "I don't have one either, but I'll ask Julian." Unless someone actually has a bicycle, you will never get one. Even if there were a million people in the chain, you still would not get your bicycle unless someone actually had one.

...there needs to be something solid at the beginning of all these causes.

Philosophers put it this way: "An infinite regress causes nothing." Something at the beginning must have the power to put all of this in motion. This first cause must be something that does not need to be caused itself nor should it depend upon anything else for its existence.

In fact, only one being possibly fits this bill – God.

Evidence from Time: How This Very Moment Demonstrates the Need for a Beginning

The cosmological argument, an argument from first cause, also

---

1   This idea is what philosophers call infinite regress.

applies to our understanding of time. Those who believe that God does not exist must think of the universe as having always existed, or they have no explanation at all. Philosophers have pointed out that it is not rational to believe that the world has always existed. Think of a number line that stretches back to infinity. Place yourself on the time line somewhere in infinity past.

∞ Past   Today   Future ∞

If we start at infinity past and travel forward on the time line 10,000 years, where would we be? Negative infinity plus 10,000 is still negative infinity ($10,000 + -\infty = -\infty$). How about if we travel forward 20 million years on this infinite time line? Where would we be? Again, you are stuck in infinity past. In fact, if the past is infinite, we would never be able to arrive at today, and yet, here we are. The most reasonable explanation for our arrival at this moment is the truth that the universe had a beginning. Scientists now agree that the correct time line of the universe looks something like this:

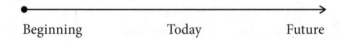

Beginning   Today   Future

If the universe had a definite beginning at a particular point in time, we must then ask what caused this beginning. The argument gets quite interesting at this point as atheists attempt to find a cause for the universe. Strange theories have arisen to attempt to avoid answering that God caused the universe. For example, one theory argues that the universe just "popped" into being for no reason at all. Another theory claims that the universe pulsates in and out of existence on a semi-regular basis. Another asserts that there are billions of universes popping in and out of existence like bubbles in a bathtub. The only thing these theories do, however, is produce new questions. Where did the billions of universes come from? What caused the pulsations? Why did we "pop" into and out of existence?

Even more troubling to the atheistic argument is the question of *why* the universe began at the exact moment that it did and not before. "Why is this a problem?" some might ask. Have you ever made a home volcano kit with vinegar and baking soda? You get all the ingredients ready and keep them separate until just the right moment. Why the need for separation? As soon as you pour the vinegar on top of the baking soda, the explosion happens. By their very nature and according to the chemical laws that govern our world, baking soda and vinegar CANNOT just float around in a bowl together without producing an explosive reaction. In the world we live in, baking soda and vinegar necessarily produce explosive results when they are combined, and it takes an intelligent being, a person, to keep them apart, and an intelligent actor to put them together. The fact that the universe began at a particular point implies that a decision-making person said, "Now!"

Again, the biblical account fits best with the evidence. In the beginning, God said, "Now!" The most reasonable explanation for the beginning of the universe and the process of time is that God caused these things to occur.

Evidence from Logic Alone: Why It Is Irrational to Claim that God Does Not Exist

In AD 1077, an intelligent monk named Saint Anselm wrote one of the most fascinating arguments for God's existence. He began with a reflection on a single verse of Scripture and from this verse developed one of the most insightful and controversial arguments of all time. He wrote his argument as a prayer, praising God for the way He made the world and the way He has made Himself known through reason. Modern philosophers are still arguing over this simple thought gleaned from a medieval monk's personal devotions. It has come to be called the ontological argument, and it is based on the belief that God is a necessary being.

The fool says in his heart, "There is no God." Anselm read from Psalm 14:1. He observed that the psalm didn't merely claim atheism[1] was wrong; it also claimed atheism was foolish. He began to consider what was foolish about the phrase, *There is no God*, and here is what he discovered.

If we are to argue about whether God exists, we must first agree on how to define God. The same would be true if we were to argue about the existence of anything: apples, horses, bowling balls, or unicorns. We must agree on what we are arguing about. So Anselm begins with this definition of God: "God is that being than which no greater being can possibly be conceived." Or put another way, God is the greatest being that can be imagined. Most would agree that this is what we mean when we say *God*, but even though many might want to add particular qualities or characteristics to God, this minimal definition seems right.

Next, Anselm notes that surely this God exists in our minds, and we are able to understand the concept, since we are here arguing about God right now. He then argues that if God exists only in our minds and does not exist in reality, then He is not the greatest imaginable being. Why not? We can imagine something greater than this being that is only in our minds – namely, the being that exists in reality. Imaginary beings are not as great as real beings. I can imagine a hundred dollars, but a real hundred-dollar bill in my pocket would be much more

---

1   **Atheism:** The belief that there is no God.

fun. Thus, in order for God to be the greatest imaginable being, God must exist in reality.

A fellow monk thought Anselm had made a mistake, since this argument sounded too simple. This monk, named Guanilo, wrote Anselm a letter called "On Behalf of the Fool." He argued that Anselm's claim meant anything could be imagined into existence. If I imagined the greatest possible island, Guanilo argued, it doesn't mean this imaginary island is real.

Anselm answered his critic by revealing that one cannot imagine the greatest possible island at all. Islands can always be improved. What if we added one more nice palm tree? How about a little better surf or a bit more sand? Furthermore, no one can even agree on what makes an island the best. Some want palm trees, some don't. Some like sand, while others are bothered by the gritty stuff. Some want music and others prefer quiet. In fact, the best possible island can't exist at all. We can, however, imagine the greatest possible being. We can even say exactly what we mean by *God*: "God is that being than which no greater being can ever be imagined." Thus, Anselm claims, Guanilo's objection fails.

...it is not even possible to rationally claim there is no God.

Many today still debate this interesting argument. Even though thinkers are divided about its validity, Anselm's argument continues to provoke challenging discussions and befuddling questions. I once attended a party for philosophers (doesn't that sound fun?) that began with the icebreaker question, "Do you believe Anselm's ontological argument works?" If the ontological argument ignited by Anselm does work, and I believe it does, it is not even possible to rationally claim *there is no God*.

Evidence from Experience: How God's Work in Our Lives Demonstrates His Involvement

Another line of evidence comes from experiences of God through miracles, answered prayer, and changed lives. Around the globe, the world resounds with story after story of miraculous and unexplainable events. We hear of healings, dramatic conversion stories, and amazing provisions. Perhaps you have seen a direct answer to prayer yourself or had an experience that convinces you of God's presence. These stories don't merely come from one group of people or from one area of the world. Instead, we find tales of experiences with God throughout all of the countries of the world and throughout all of history.

When my older sister was preparing to go to college, my family did not have the funds she needed. My father invited us to pray for the required amount in order to reserve a spot for my sister. We gathered on the floor of our den and asked God to provide the $250 fee. We asked God to guide my sister, to show her whether this college was the right choice. While we were still kneeling on the floor praying, someone knocked at the front door. My dad went to answer the door and found the mailman standing there with a piece of registered mail all the way from Sweden. "Would you sign for this, sir?" he asked.

My dad signed for the mail and read the return address. "I haven't heard from these people in fifteen years!" he exclaimed. He brought the letter in to where we had been praying and opened it. The long-lost friends had written a greeting and sent a check as a gift. Can you guess the amount of the check? They had sent exactly $250 in U.S. dollars!

We find another amazing account in the book *Unbroken*, written about the famous World War II veteran Louis Zamperini. A *New York Times* best seller, this book has inspired millions with the true story of Zamperini's plane crash, his survival in a life raft on the open ocean for forty-seven days, his terrifying experiences as a prisoner of war, and his subsequent rescue. Near the end of the book, the author explains how Zamperini had been psychologically damaged by all of these life events. Nightmares, alcohol abuse, and outbursts of fear and anger plagued him. One evening, his wife convinced him to attend a Billy Graham crusade where he heard the gospel. Though he initially resisted, God worked on his heart, reminding him of a desperate prayer he had made on the life raft, asking God to save him. When Zamperini finally gave his life to Jesus, the nightmares ceased, and his alcoholism had no more power over him. He ultimately returned to Japan, the scene of his own imprisonment and torture, as an evangelist.

While not everyone receives such tangible answers to prayer or miraculous manifestations of deliverance, the world is full of stories that demonstrate the power and presence of God in the lives of people. How are we to account for these dramatic testimonies? We could argue that all of these stories are coincidence. We could attempt to show that all of them are deceptions. We could try to find other ways to explain each story, reinterpreting all of the events according to naturalistic causes. But would that be rational? The most reasonable explanation for the vast number of stories of God's intervention is that God exists, and from time to time He intervenes in the world.

Evidence from Morality: How Our Knowledge of Right and Wrong is Evidence of God's Existence

Why does everyone seem to know what is right and what is wrong? While we may argue over particular instances and particular moral theories, we all seem to agree on the basics. Lying, stealing, murder, and cheating are wrong. Telling the truth, generosity, saving lives, and being honest are right.[1]

---

1   Most ethicists argue for a hierarchy within these moral absolutes. While most people agree that murder and lying are both wrong, most would also say that murder is a greater evil than lying. So if faced with the choice of lying to prevent a murder or

These truths are almost universally accepted by all cultures as right and good. We don't think these things are just useful or pleasing to us; we know them to be morally right for all people in all places at all times. Even more to the point, we recognize that these things are wrong or right for anyone anywhere. Philosophers call these truths moral absolutes or moral facts.

Where do these moral facts come from? If there is no God, we must find a naturalistic or scientific explanation for them. This is impossible, however, since moral truths cannot be explained in the language of physics, chemistry, or biology. No physical law governs the fact that it is wrong to steal. We can't find the fact that murder is wrong under a microscope or isolate it with a Bunsen burner. Yet everyone still seems to know it.

Imagine if God were not real and we were all merely complex animals fighting for our own survival. Wouldn't it be more reasonable for us to exalt selfishness over sacrifice and stealing over giving? It would make sense that if no God existed, it would be fine to lie, cheat, and steal if these helped us to survive. Think of a time when someone stole something from you or unfairly took your place in line or lied to you. Was your first reaction, "Wow! They are excellent survivors! Maybe I should be more like them." No, we don't naturally think like that. More than likely our first reaction would be one of anger over the injustice we had experienced.

One evening, I forgot to lock my car. To make matters worse, I left my bag with books and my computer inside the car. In the morning, I discovered a crime scene on my driveway. The contents of the glove compartment lay strewn about the front seat, the doors were opened, and the bag had disappeared. My books and computer were gone. In a wonderful twist of irony, the perpetrator stole my Bible and a book entitled *Moral Choices*

telling the truth and being reasonably certain that a murder would result, the moral obligation is to tell a lie in order to prevent a greater evil.

along with my computer. The criminal ditched the *Moral Choices* book just a few houses down the road, but made off with the Bible and computer. Obviously, thinking about right and wrong did not appeal to the criminal at that particular time. Were the criminal's actions merely part of a different standard? Were they okay for him but merely inconvenient to me? No, the actions were wrong.

The Bible explains that knowledge of right and wrong is instilled within us, and when we choose to ignore this knowledge, we sin. Paul wrote that even those who have never seen the Ten Commandments know what is right and wrong. *Indeed, when Gentiles, who do not have the law, do by nature things required by the law, they are a law for themselves, even though they do not have the law. They show that the requirements of the law are written on their hearts.*[1]

The most rational explanation for a person's knowledge of right and wrong is that this is how God has designed people.

Conclusion

When I was in high school, I often discussed with friends my belief in God's existence. Our English classes provided fertile ground for these discussions. As Camus or Faulkner waxed eloquent in our reading assignments, our classroom discussions returned again and again to whether there could be a God. One friend loved to take the atheist position and defend the case against God. Yet when we were seniors, he came to me one afternoon with a confession: "I now see that it takes me just as much faith to be an atheist as it takes you to be a Christian."

---

1   Romans 2:14-15.

His comment demonstrated his weakening trust in a position without solid evidence. Why would you step off the cliff of atheism and trust a weak strand of evidence with nothing to gain in eternity for your efforts? Peter Kreeft puts it this way: "Atheism is a terrible bet. It gives you no chance of winning the prize."[1]

...it takes me just as much faith to be an atheist as it takes you to be a Christian.

Pause and consider the vast amount of evidence that God has left in this world: evidence from design in nature, from first causes, from time, from logic, from experience, and from the knowledge of right and wrong. When considered as a full, cumulative case, the evidence is overwhelming and the conclusion is clear. It is far more reasonable to believe that God exists and has designed the world to reflect His presence.

Discussion Questions

- What evidence for God's existence seems the strongest to you and why? What evidence seems weaker or more difficult to understand?

- When considering all the evidence together, how strong do you think the case for God's existence is? Do you think there are other possible answers that could fit all of the evidence together?

- How would those opposed to God's existence attempt to answer each piece of evidence? What objections might they raise? How would an atheist account for origins, design in the universe, the presence of morality, and religious experience?

- Is it possible to *know* that God exists? Or must one take it on faith? What does it mean to have faith?

---

1   Peter Kreeft, "The Argument from Pascal's Wager," *www.peterkreeft.com/topics/ pascals-wager.htm.*

Chapter 3

Is the Bible Trustworthy?

By Dennis B. Moles

The message on her voice mail was brief: "Hey! I'm home for my semester break. Want to grab coffee at our usual spot? I really need to talk." Linda recognized Makayla's voice right away. Makayla had been in Linda's church small group during her four years of high school, and even though she was now away at college, they still kept in touch.

The next day the two ladies sank into a couple of secluded coffeehouse comfy chairs and began to catch up on their lives. After a few minutes of small talk over sips of espresso, Linda asked Makayla what was on her mind.

"Well, I think I might be losing my faith. The doubts started at the beginning of my freshman year, and recently they've gotten much worse. I thought if I just prayed more and read my Bible every day, they would go away, but they haven't."

Over the next two hours, Makayla talked and Linda listened. And the more she talked, the more Linda became convinced that the main source of her struggle was the Bible. Makayla just wasn't sure she could trust it anymore. Her doubts and pressing questions about the trustworthiness of the Bible came to full bloom in the last semester when she took a literature course titled "World Mythologies." In this class, the professor spent two full weeks presenting a series of lectures titled "The Bible – Mythic History or Historic Myth?"

During this series of lectures, her professor made three statements that troubled her:

> *"There is no significant historical or archeological evidence to support the accuracy of the Bible."*

> *"There is very little textual evidence to support the claims of the Bible aside from a few ancient and inconsistent scraps."*

> *"Modern science has disproven the Bible."*

"I suppose," Makayla concluded, "I just want to know how you deal with it. How do you keep on believing the Bible when there are so many problems with it?"

How would you respond to the claims made by Makayla's professor? Is what he said true? These types of claims are not just high-sounding academic thoughts; they shape people's worldviews. Often people doubt the existence or character of the God of the Bible because they doubt the Bible. It is critical that a person takes the time to examine the evidence regarding the trustworthiness of Scripture.

This chapter will present three things to help you understand the trustworthiness of the Bible, as well as give you tools to converse with others on this topic:

1. This chapter will help you know where to start a conversation with others.

2. This chapter will present responses with evidence to the doubts raised by Makayla's professor.

3. Finally, this chapter will show that the Bible offers answers to life's biggest questions.

Starting in the Right Place

Imagine having a discussion with a friend who believes that the *New York Times* is inaccurate and an untrustworthy source of information. Your friend tells you that he believes everyone at the *Times* is corrupt and that the paper is unreliable. You disagree with this assessment and set out to build a case for the dependability of the *Times*. Imagine how your friend would respond if you began your argument by saying, "According to the *New York Times,* newspapers are fifty percent more likely to be accurate than Internet news sources." Would this line of reasoning convince a skeptical person of the trustworthiness of the *Times*? Probably not.

Many Christians do not struggle with doubts regarding the trustworthiness of the Bible. They assume it is reliable because they believe the Bible is inspired by God. Theologically, this is commendable and an appropriate view of Scripture, but it will not convince the skeptic. Similar to the *New York Times* example above, when a person uses the Bible to prove the Bible's trustworthiness, little headway is made with the doubter. This does not mean there is no internal evidence for the reliability of the Scriptures. There is quite a bit: fulfilled prophecy, consistency and progress of the message, and the way it presents its heroes.[1] What it does mean is that Christians who want to undergird their own faith in the Bible or be effective in convincing others of its trustworthiness should also look to evidences outside the Bible. In fact, when it comes to apologetic[2] discussions with a person who does

It is critical that a person takes the time to examine the evidence...

---

[1] Most other religious texts do not present the flaws and failings of their heroes the way the Bible does. The Scriptures tell us that Abraham lied and told Pharaoh Sarai was his sister and not his wife (Genesis 12:10-13); David power-raped Bathsheba and then plotted the murder of her husband Uriah to cover up his sin (2 Samuel 11, 12); and Peter was rebuked by the Lord and called a devil (Matthew 16:23; Mark 8:33).

[2] **Apologetics**: The discipline of defending a position or body of doctrines. In regards

not trust the Bible, the best starting place is to present reasons to trust Scripture from outside the Bible's claims about itself.

How Do We Know What We Know?

A Christian holds that the Bible is the inspired Word of God, but this belief cannot be empirically proven beyond all doubt. In other words, a person cannot evaluate the trustworthiness of the Bible with their five senses (smell, touch, taste, hearing, or sight). Thankfully, science and firsthand experience are not the only ways to discover truth and gain knowledge.[1]

One reason some struggle to acknowledge that the Bible is uniquely authored by God is due to the epistemological question, "How do we know what we know?" If knowing something is true requires that I have empirical proof as a result of scientific testing, then I will never arrive at a biblical view of Scripture. So what are our options? Can we claim knowledge that is based on reasonable evaluation of the evidence available? Can we know things that we don't experience firsthand or have scientific proof of?

To address these questions, consider the following statements:

I love my spouse.

The sunset is beautiful.

Abraham Lincoln was the sixteenth president of the United States.

Is it reasonable to say that I can *know* each of these statements is true? Some may protest that the first two claims are subjective because they are based on what a person feels or what they believe to be true. In contrast, we can objectively

---

to Christian theology, apologetics is the task of defending or explaining Christian faith.

1   For a robust explanation of knowledge, see chapter 1, "Can We Know What We Believe?"

know that Lincoln was our sixteenth president, because it can be verified by evidence. But is this really the case?

I know that no one who is reading this book was alive to vote for Lincoln in either 1860 or 1864. Yet without this firsthand experience, an abundance of documents such as books, letters, and photos still exist that concur Lincoln was the sixteenth president. But what if, in the face of overwhelming evidence to the contrary, I remained committed to my unbelief and ardently refused to accept that Honest Abe was Commander-in-Chief from 1861 to 1865? I suppose most people would be shocked by my skepticism because of the amount of evidence available to know that Lincoln was who history says he was. Mountains of evidence confirm that he was elected in 1860, reelected in 1864, signed the Emancipation Proclamation on January 1, 1863, and was assassinated by John Wilkes Booth on April 14, 1865. The fact is, historical evidence from many reputable sources in the 1850s and 1860s makes it impossible to deny that Abraham Lincoln was the sixteenth president of the United States.

...a person cannot evaluate the trustworthiness of the Bible with their five senses...

This example demonstrates that although we cannot prove by firsthand experience or scientific testing that Lincoln was president, we can still have knowledge that this happened. We must admit that it is possible to be wrong about this, but due to the abundance of evidence, the chances of this are astronomically small. Therefore, because of our level of confidence in the evidence, we have legitimate reasons to hold our belief. We arrive at most of what we know in this manner, whether we are talking about what we ate for dinner last night or how we invest in the stock market. The goal is never trying to possess bombproof certainty in what we know, particularly when it comes to the Bible. The goal is to follow the evidence where it leads and draw appropriate conclusions about what is reasonable to believe.

So where does the evidence lead when it comes to the reliability of the Bible? Again, was Makayla's professor correct in his claims? To make a case that the Bible is trustworthy and should be read and obeyed, I will address each of the protests made by the professor to see where the evidence leads.

Protest #1

There is no significant historical or archeological evidence to support the accuracy of the Bible.

At the turn of the twentieth century, archaeologist John Garstang made a shattering discovery: He found archaeological evidence for the Hittite empire. The significance of this discovery centered on the reliability of the Bible, which mentions the Hittite people. Although the Hittites are referenced in other pieces of ancient literature,[1] the lack of solid archeological evidence up to that point had caused many scholars in the late 1800s to call into question the historicity and reliability of Scripture. But when Garstang made his discovery in 1908, this information quieted the skeptics on their critique of the Bible, at least regarding the existence of the Hittites.

Other biblical claims have also been verified archeologically and historically. For example, the Taylor Prism[2] confirms the Assyrian siege of Jerusalem that the Bible describes in 2 Kings 18-19, 2 Chronicles 32, and Isaiah 36-37. The excavation of the Tel Dan Stele confirms the historicity of Israel's King David.[3] The nineteenth-century discoveries of the Cyrus Cylinder and

---

1   Miriam Lichtheim, *Ancient Egyptian Literature: Volume II: The New Kingdom* (Berkeley, CA: University of California Press, 2006), 57.

2   This six-sided clay cylinder was discovered during an excavation of the biblical city of Nineveh and dates from 705 to 681 BC. The Taylor Prism mentions King Hezekiah by name.

3   E. M. Blaiklick and R. K. Harrison, *The New International Dictionary of Biblical Archaeology* (Grand Rapids, MI: Zondervan, 1983), 436-437.

the Moabite Stone also support the historical accuracy of the Bible. The Cyrus Cylinder records Cyrus the Persian's decree that allowed Babylonian captives to return to their homes and resume their religious practices after the exile.[1] The Moabite Stone was discovered in Dhiban, four miles north of the River Arnon, and substantiates the events of 2 Kings 3. It even mentions significant names: the Moabite King Mesha[2] and Yahweh.[3]

Historical documents also verify the truthfulness of the Bible's content and production. Jewish historian Josephus and Roman historian Tacitus both testify to the historicity of Jesus.[4] Josephus even mentions Jesus' miracles and resurrection. Bithynian Governor Pliny the Younger stated that the Christians in his province maintained their belief in and worship of Jesus even when faced with death.[5] And Irenaeus, a second-century church father, has this to say about the biblical Gospels themselves:

> "Matthew also issued a written Gospel among
> the Hebrews in their own dialect, while Peter
> and Paul were preaching at Rome, and laying the
> foundations of the Church. After their departure,
> Mark, the disciple and interpreter of Peter, did
> also hand down to us in writing what had been
> preached by Peter. Luke also, the companion of
> Paul, recorded in a book the Gospel preached by
> him. Afterwards, John, the disciple of the Lord,

---

1 Ibid., 146. This artifact substantiates the claims made in Ezra 1:1-3; 6:3; 2 Chronicles 36:23; and Isaiah 44:28. It is housed in the British Museum.

2 2 Kings 3:4 – "Now Mesha king of Moab raised sheep, and he had to pay the king of Israel a tribute of a hundred thousand lambs and the wool of a hundred thousand rams. But after Ahab died, the king of Moab rebelled against the king of Israel."

3 Blaiklick and Harrison, *The New International Dictionary of Biblical Archaeology*, 409. See also *www.jewish encyclopedia.com/articles/10899-moabite-stone*. The Moabite Stone can be seen in the Louvre.

4 William Whiston, ed., trans., *The Works of Josephus: Updated Edition, Complete and Unabridged* (Peabody, MA: Hendrickson Publishers, 1987).

5 Doug Powell, *Holman QuickSource Guide to Christian Apologetics* (Nashville, TN: Holman Reference, 2006), 164-166.

who also had leaned upon His breast, did himself
publish a Gospel during his residence at Ephesus
in Asia."[1]

While these examples are a small sampling of the available
information supporting the Bible's accuracy, they are sufficient
to disprove the assertion that no significant historical or archaeological evidence exists to support the accuracy of the Bible.

Protest #2

*There is very little textual evidence to support the claims of the
Bible aside from a few ancient and inconsistent scraps.*

This protest against the Bible is easily overturned when
examining the evidence. The Christian Scriptures are the most
thoroughly attested documents in the history of literature. This
may seem like a bold claim, but three simple criteria support
it: the historical distance between the original writing and the
oldest possessed copies, the number of known and documented
copies, and the consistency among the copies.

For many years, opponents of biblical trustworthiness cited
the historical distance between the original and the current
available manuscripts. The scholars who held to the trustworthiness of the Bible reasoned that the meticulous attention to
detail by the scriptural scribes and copyists made it reasonable
to believe that the documents that had been copied and handed
down through the ages were accurate representations of the
originals. Those who did not accept this contention argued that
historical distance necessarily equated mistakes. They argued
that the historical distance between the original writing and
the oldest existing copies made it impossible to know if the
current copies actually represented the originals.

---

1   Alexander Roberts, D.D., James Donaldson, LL.D., and A. Cleveland Coxe, eds.,
     "Irenaeus: Against Heresies," *The Ante-Nicene Fathers, Volume I: The Apostolic
     Fathers with Justin Martyr and Irenaeus* (Buffalo, NY: Christian Literature
     Company, 1885), 414.

This argument suffered a crippling blow after the discovery of the Dead Sea Scrolls in the late 1940s to the mid-1950s. The Dead Sea Scrolls are a collection of over 950 text fragments or manuscripts. Most of these texts are copies of the Old Testament Scriptures that date from the third century BC to the mid-first century AD. Until this discovery, the earliest known textual manuscript from the Old Testament was the Masoretic Text (MT), which dated from about AD 980. Not only did the Dead Sea Scrolls provide additional ancient copies of the Old Testament, but they also allowed scholars to investigate the consistency between earlier and later copies. What they found was stunning.

When comparing the MT copy of Isaiah 53 and copies of the same passage found in the Dead Sea Scrolls (part of the Qumran Sectarian Manuscripts or QSM), the consistency was striking. Even though these documents were separated by approximately a thousand years, the scholars discovered that the differences between the QSM and the MT were miniscule, effectively disproving the claim that *significant* scribal mistakes and changes were inevitable. This same pattern of consistency between the Dead Sea Scrolls and the MT was found throughout the ancient artifacts.

The discovery of the Dead Sea Scrolls gave tangible evidence to the accuracy claims Christian and Jewish scholars have been making for years. Consider the following example from a comparison of Isaiah 53 cited above: Out of the 166 Hebrew words in Isaiah 53, only seventeen letters differ between the QSM and MT, and none of these spelling or stylistic changes have any effect on biblical teaching. This comparison demonstrates the great care taken in the copying and preservation of the biblical text.[1]

---

1   Norman L. Geisler and William E. Nix, *A General Introduction to the Bible* (Chicago, IL: Moody Press, 1986), 196, 261-270, 351-385.

Next, Homer wrote *The Iliad* in approximately 800 BC, and 643 known Greek copies or portions of copies are still in existence. The earliest of these is a partial copy that dates to approximately 400 BC, while the first complete text dates to the thirteenth century. This means there is an historical distance of around 400 years between the actual writing of *The Iliad* and the earliest documentation.

It may come as a surprise, but the 400-year historical distance is quite short, and 643 known copies is quite a large number when we compare it with the numbers of copies and the years of historical distance of other ancient works. For example, eight copies of Herodotus's *The Histories* exist, and the historical distance between original and early copy is 1,350 years. Only ten copies of Caesar's *The Gallic Wars* exist, and the historical distance is 1,000 years. There are just twenty copies of Tacitus's *Annals*, seven copies of Pliny Secundus's *Natural History*, and twenty copies of Livy's *History of Rome* with historical distances that are 1,000 years, 750 years, and 400 years, respectively.[1]

Given this information, one would think that if the manuscript evidence for New Testament documents approaches that of *The Iliad*, it would bolster our belief that the Bible is trustworthy. Currently there are approximately 5,500 full or partial copies of the New Testament, and an entire copy of the New Testament can be dated to within 225 years of the original writing. The oldest confirmed copies of the New Testament Scriptures date back to AD 114. This means that the historical distance between our oldest copies and the date of the original writing is at most fifty years. I say *at most* because of a recent discovery by Dr. Dan Wallace and his team of researchers from The Center for the Study of New Testament Manuscripts. Dr.

---

1   Josh McDowell, *The New Evidence That Demands a Verdict* (Nashville, TN: Thomas Nelson, 1999), 38.

Wallace believes that his team has located a text fragment from the gospel of Mark that dates back to the first century.[1]

When we compare the textual evidence for the Christian Scriptures with the textual evidence for other ancient works, there is, frankly, no comparison. The Scriptures are the most thoroughly researched and attested document in the history of literature.[2]

Protest #3
Modern science has disproven the Bible.

Many people find it impossible to accept the Bible as true because they cannot reconcile the miracles in the Bible with what they understand to be possible from modern science. This is a result of their naturalistic worldview. This view of the world assumes that things are not real or knowable unless they are composed of matter or energy and can be tested and measured scientifically.[3] They reason that we can only know and trust things that we know scientifically or have experienced. This view is also called scientism.[4] For this reason, many naturalistic thinkers believe modern science has disproven the Bible. They reason that since the Bible's miracle claims are scientifically impossible, the Bible must be false.

They reason that we can only know and trust things that we know scientifically...

Several years ago, I pastored a small church in central Ohio. During that time, my wife, Amy, and I met Chris and Kathy.

---

1   Daniel B. Wallace, "Earliest Manuscript of the New Testament Discovered?" The Center for the Study of New Testament Manuscripts: *www.csntm.org/News/Archive/2012/2/10/EarliestManuscriptoftheNewTestamentDiscovered* (February 10, 2012).

2   Daniel B. Wallace, "The Bible: Why Does It Endure?" (A Day of Discovery video), Our Daily Bread Ministries: *dod.org/programs/the-bible-why-does-it-endure-part-i/* (2011).

3   Notice that this claim says only what is real and knowable can be tested scientifically, yet the claim itself cannot be tested in this way because it is a philosophical proposition. The very definition of scientism asks you not to believe it is true.

4   **Scientism**: The view that only science is able to provide knowledge (strong scientism) or is the best source for knowledge (weak scientism). See chapter 6, "What Is a Worldview and Why Does It Matter?" for a fuller treatment of scientism.

Chris and Kathy are two of the brightest and kindest people I have ever met. They both taught in the biology department at a local college – each holding a Ph.D. from a prestigious Ivy League university. Our two sons and their two sons attended the same elementary school, and as our boys became fast friends, so did we. Chris and I would often meet for coffee to discuss, challenge, and learn from one another in the areas of science and religion. But it was a conversation with Kathy that remains one of the most profound I have ever had.

The birthday party for our youngest son was in full swing. Close to a dozen kindergarteners had shown up to help him celebrate. In the middle of this barely controlled chaos, Kathy, whose son was among the sugar-fueled hoard, turned to Amy and me and said, "I have a question, but I don't want to offend you." After assuring her that we were hard to offend, she slowly and deliberately said, "Amy, you're a nurse. And you both still believe in the virgin birth?"

For Kathy, this was a real and well-intended question. How could two reasonably bright people, one with a college degree in science, believe that a virgin could have a baby? Kathy was not trying to trap us or drag us into a debate; she was genuinely wondering how we could reconcile holding two seemingly contradictory beliefs.

In this moment, Amy and I did two things that surprised our friend. First, we affirmed her skepticism by saying we also believe that it is *scientifically* impossible for a virgin to have a baby. Second, we tried to answer the real question that lurked just behind her question. How can you trust a truth source (the Bible) that contradicts another – and in her view more-reliable – truth source (reproductive science)?

We told her that we believed in the virgin birth not just because the Bible said it happened, but also because we believe that the God of the Bible *could* make it happen. This may seem like a cop-out – to say that God can do anything He wants – but it is really the crux of the issue. We believe something that is impossible to explain scientifically can still happen because God can make it so. Christians who hold to the trustworthiness of the Bible are not the only ones who hold beliefs that are scientifically impossible.

When it comes to the origin of the universe, atheistic naturalists hold a belief that contradicts science. They believe that something – everything actually – came from nothing. They claim that life emerged as a result of time and chance with no causal agent. They not only claim that life emerged from non-life, but also that life and non-life sprang from nothingness. Noted atheist Richard Dawkins feels so strongly about this "something from nothing" doctrine that he repeatedly reminds his readers that the universe is a completely random place. Why does he do this? He dogmatically clings to the belief that there cannot be a design because of his deeply held belief that there is no designer. If there is design, there must be a designer. So no matter how fine-tuned the universe appears, it must be a random place if there is no God.

Why does this matter? It matters because all of us, at some level, believe things that cannot be proven scientifically. It matters because all of us make faith assumptions, even if our faith is in science, to give us answers to all of our questions. Even Makayla's professor's assertion that science has disproven the Bible is a faith statement rooted in the belief that miracles are impossible because God does not exist.

Bible believers do not disbelieve the laws of nature any more than the atheist does who insists everything came from nothing. Bible believers affirm natural law and the truths science can teach. They are the rules God has established for the world to function. Virgins don't have babies, except for that one time when God needed a virgin to have a baby, so He could save the world from sin. We can believe this happened because God, the maker of the laws of nature, has the prerogative and power to work outside of the laws He established. If there is no God, there can be no miracles; if there are no miracles, then virgins don't have babies, and something can never come from nothing. And if something cannot come from nothing, then the naturalist has no way of explaining how we all got here in the first place.

...science is simply not the right tool for testing certain truth-claims.

Many people face this dilemma. How can they trust the Bible when its miracle claims stretch their worldview beyond its limits? How can they trust something that seems to fail the simplest scientific testing?

As we discovered earlier, sometimes we know things are true that cannot be scientifically proven. In some cases, science is simply not the right tool for testing certain truth-claims. I know things that I cannot prove, but I don't know them any less than things I can prove scientifically. I know that torturing babies for fun is wrong in all social contexts, but I have no scientific data to substantiate that moral conviction because science cannot explain morality. I know that 2 + 2 = 4, but I cannot prove that scientifically either; science assumes mathematical truths in order to function, but it cannot prove mathematics. And most intriguing, I cannot scientifically validate the scientific method. Even the statement "science has disproven the Bible" is a faith observation that cannot be proven scientifically.

Has science disproven the Bible? No. Science simply tells us that there is no natural explanation for some of the Bible's truth-claims. But when we think about it, there are no natural or scientific explanations for love either, yet no one would say that science has disproven love. It's just not something science can do.

The Bible Offers Answers to Life's Big Questions

As humans, we seem to have an inherent desire to inquire, question, and discover. We are not satisfied to simply exist, but we seem to have something within us causing us to explore and create in a special and distinct way. Sooner or later, most people start to look for answers to some of life's big questions. We look into the night sky and wonder, "Where did all this come from?" We stand beside the hospital bed of a sick child and can't help but ask, "Why is the world so messed up?" Many of us lay awake at night considering, "Is there really any meaning and purpose in this life?" And all of us, sooner or later, ponder the question, "What happens to us when we die?"

I've been acquainted with the Bible all of my life. I've read its stories; I've learned the languages it was originally written in; I've studied the history surrounding it and the theology[1] that has arisen from it. The Bible is intricate, complex, and ancient. But it is also the most honest, applicable, and life-changing text in existence. And it offers the most compelling, rational, and consistent answers to life's big questions than any other religious text or worldview.

Where did all this come from?

The Bible's account of creation serves as a lucid and rational basis for morality, beauty, goodness, and an ordered universe. It answers the question of how everything came into existence; an all-powerful and loving God created it. The Bible's answer to, "Where did all this come from?" avoids the problem of infinite regress by presenting God as the non-created, self-sustaining, and foundational being who is the first and necessary mover of everything.[2]

The Bible not only tells us that God created and sustains

---

1   Theology: The study of God.
2   Genesis 1:1-2:25.

everything, but it also tells us that because He is good and benevolent, everything He created was good.[1] Because humans have been created in the image of this moral and good God, they are capable of distinguishing between right and wrong, beautiful and offensive, and good and evil. Good and evil are not social constructs but are determined by the unchanging Creator who shows us what goodness looks like.

Without a Creator, we are left with a universe that popped into existence from nothing with no causal agent. And without a good and loving Creator, we have no explanation for morality or beauty. The Bible offers an answer to the question, "Where did all this come from?" that is consistent with reality and serves as a basis for morality, beauty, and scientific inquiry.

Why is the world so messed up?

The earth is full of wonders: beautiful sunsets, majestic mountains, and expansive oceans. But it is also filled with pain, suffering, abuse, and evil. Some assert that the existence of evil and suffering prove there is either no God or that God is not good. Again, the Bible offers an answer to this question. It tells us that God created the world good, but sin, which was introduced by our first parents, Adam and Eve, has broken and continues to break this good world.

The Bible tells us the world is messed up because of sin. God did not create sin, neither is He responsible for it. Cancer, abuse, famine, pestilence, and even natural disasters are all indicators that the world is desperately in need of fixing. And the Scriptures tell us the world is messed up because we have separated ourselves from our loving and gracious Creator, and the consequence of that separation is a world run amuck.[2]

---

1   Genesis 1:25, 31.
2   See chapter 9, "Why Would a Good God Allow Suffering?" for more on this topic.

Is there any meaning or purpose in this life?

The third question that plagues all of us is the question of meaning. If there is no God, then we truly do live in a random and harsh world. Everything we see would have come about by accident, and there would be no basis for morality, beauty, or philanthropy. If naturalism[1] is true, then the world with all of its evil, disease, death, and poverty *is* the best it can be. If this is the case, then my only job is to live as long as I can, as comfortably as I can. Surviving day by day and ascending the food chain becomes the most meaningful thing I can hope to accomplish in this harsh and unforgiving world.

But the Bible paints a different picture of reality for us. It not only tells us that an all-powerful and perfectly loving God created everything that exists, but it also tells us that this God is in the business of redeeming and restoring everything that has been broken and affected by sin.[2]

God created, humans sinned, the world and everything in it was broken, but God refused to allow His good creation to stay broken and estranged from Him. The Bible tells us that God, in the person of Jesus Christ, came to earth to defeat sin, conquer death, and give us hope. Jesus pushed back the effects of sin, offering forgiveness, healing the sick, feeding the hungry, and showing mercy to the wicked and marginalized. Jesus came into the world to fix what sin had broken and to break the hold sin had on humanity.

Life has purpose because Jesus has given it purpose. The Bible tells us that after Jesus rose from the dead, He gave His followers a mission to fulfill. He told them to go throughout the world as His representative and carry on His mission of making disciples of all nations, which can be characterized as

---

1   **Naturalism**: A philosophical view that holds that everything in existence arises from natural properties and causes and anything supernatural or spiritual, including God, does not exist.

2   Colossians 1:20.

mending what sin has wrecked and breaking the strongholds of sin in the lives of people.[1]

Our life has meaning because what we do matters. Our actions have significance and our choices really do count. From the Bible we learn God has invited people to join Him in His work around the world. The opportunities to serve God as we serve others are not only a mark of obedience, but also a privilege to be a part of the Lord's work. In this way, our life has meaning and our efforts have eternal consequences.

Where do I find hope?

The Bible doesn't just tell us where we come from; it also tells us where we are going. The Bible is a story of God's love and redemptive pursuit of His wayward creation. The same all-powerful and perfectly loving God who created everything will restore all things in the end. He did not just take our sin so we could be better people. Jesus died, was buried, and rose again, so we could be reunited with God.[2] He who took our sins on Himself at the cross demonstrated power over the most powerful and permanent effect of sin and death when He rose from the dead.

The God who created in the beginning and redeemed us at the cross will be the God who meets us in the end. This God is not petty, cruel, tame, or forgetful. He cannot tolerate sin, but He is merciful and kind to all who come to Him. And He has made a way through Jesus for all to be reconciled to Him.

The Bible tells us that we are going somewhere. Apart from Jesus, we are going away from Him; in Jesus, we are headed toward perfect reconciliation with the God who made us and has bought us back.

---

1   Matthew 28:17-20; 2 Corinthians 5:16-21.
2   Revelation 21:1-8.

Conclusion

I *know* I love my wife. I *know* a beautiful sunset when I see one. I *know* that Abraham Lincoln was the sixteenth president of the United States. And I *know* that the Bible is true and, therefore, trustworthy. Do I have questions? Sure. But faith isn't the absence of doubts or questions; it is the persistence of belief in the midst of possible doubts or questions.

If you came to this chapter looking for bombproof certainty and ironclad arguments, I'm afraid you may have been disappointed. I cannot prove beyond all *possible* doubt that the Bible is worthy of your trust and belief any more than I can prove that Abraham Lincoln was the sixteenth president of the United States. But I think we have seen that the challenges Makayla's professor leveled against the Bible simply are not true. The Bible is historically and archeologically verifiable. It is the most thoroughly attested piece of literature in human history. Science has not disproven the Bible any more than it has disproven love or beauty. And in addition to all these pieces of evidence, the Bible offers lucid and hope-filled answers to life's biggest questions. These reasons allow us to hold the conviction that the Bible is worthy of our trust.

> *Science has not disproven the Bible any more than it has disproven love or beauty.*

Discussion Questions

- Have you ever been asked any of these questions (or other questions) about the trustworthiness of the Bible?

- Which reason(s) listed in this chapter do you find most compelling to trust the Bible?

- What area do you need to give more thought to?

- Do you agree that it is possible to know something that cannot be scientifically proven?

Chapter 4

Do Moral Absolutes Exist?

By Doug Arendsee and Ryan P. Whitson

Stealing is immoral, murder is wrong, and telling a lie is unacceptable. It is possible, maybe even common, that two people could affirm these statements and yet not agree with each other.

In our day, morality is a topic most Americans recognize and consider important but struggle to understand. This is especially true when people give an ethical opinion about a moral action or thought; though they may say the same the words (for example, "murder is wrong"), they are not necessarily saying the same thing.

Consider the example of stealing with two fictional characters. Both Jeff and Sue believe taking something that belongs to another is immoral. But a closer look at *why* Jeff and Sue hold their respective views on stealing reveals an important difference. Jeff grounds his view on a complex mix of personal feelings, cultural pressure, and the law, but he rejects the idea that stealing is wrong for any ultimate or binding reasons. Therefore, when pressed if it is immoral to steal bread when hungry or lift music when low on money, Jeff may comfortably make allowances to his view, because it provides him with freedom to create his own moral preferences.

In contrast, Sue affirms stealing is wrong because she believes an absolute truth and a binding moral law exist. She believes morality is not an individual or cultural creation, but mankind depends on scientific laws to understand the physical ways of the world and moral laws to shape what it means to live a flourishing human life. Sue would be the first to admit she is not perfect in obeying the moral laws she supports, but she realizes she does not have the authority to *create* morality.

Here is why this matters. Sue represents a neglected vision of morality that believes right and wrong are rooted in the existence of some absolute truth. Jeff, on the other hand, represents those who retain the word *moral* but strip it of any authoritative meaning. This latter approach, often labeled as relativism or postmodernism, illustrates a belief that an individual or culture may determine what is ethical. While this view may come across as moral emancipation (freedom to express and experiment, freedom from guilt, and freedom from ultimate accountability and judgment), our nation should be forewarned: It may taste sweet in the mouth, but it will soon sour in the stomach.[1]

Whether or not moral absolutes exist is critically important. In this chapter, three fundamental questions will be addressed:

1. Are there moral absolutes?

2. If moral absolutes exist, can a person know what they are?

3. If moral absolutes exist, what are they?

To best unpack this topic, the second question above will be addressed first.

---

1 Ryan P. Whitson, "Concept: Pitching the Baby, Keeping the Bathwater: The Removal of Moral Absolutes," *Media Ethics Magazine*, Vol. 24, No. 1 (Fall 2012), *www.media-ethicsmagazine.com/index.php/browse-back-issues/144-fall-2012/3998648-concept-pitching-the-baby-keeping-the-bathwater-the-removal-of-moral-absolutes.*

If Moral Absolutes Exist, Can a Person Know What They Are?

In the eighteenth century, John Godfrey Saxe wrote "The Blind Men and the Elephant" based on earlier versions of the story. In the classic poem, six blind men try to describe an elephant based on the part they each touch. Each blind man is adamant about the nature of the elephant. One declares the elephant is like a tree because he has touched the leg, but another declares the elephant is like a rope because he has touched the tail. Each is logical and consistent with his experience but is wrong because of incomplete knowledge. The poem concludes:

> And so these men of Indostan
> Disputed loud and long,
> Each in his own opinion
> Exceeding stiff and strong,
> Though each was partly in the right,
> And all were in the wrong![1]

This famous poem has been interpreted a number of ways, though most agree that all people are like the blind person trying to know the real nature of truth (the elephant in the poem). The point being made is that because all are blind and no one blind person can know the complete nature of the elephant, which is often paradoxical, we conclude a person cannot ever have an accurate picture of truth. Others simply deny truth exists at all. For this reason, they stop looking for absolute truth and focus on the inadequacies of blind men's knowledge instead.

What is sometimes forgotten or ignored is that no one seeks truth in a vacuum. If all the blind men in the poem keep to themselves, they will have knowledge about some aspect of the

---

1   John Godfrey Saxe, "The Blind Men and the Elephant," *www.allaboutphilosophy. org/blind-men-and-the-elephant.htm* (July 6, 2015).

elephant, but they will be mistaken about the full nature of the animal. However, if these same blind men share their knowledge with one another, the group of them will be able to put together a fairly accurate understanding of what the elephant is like.

Now, consider a seeing person who has studied and written a book about the elephant. After listening to the book being read to them, the blind men could correlate their experience with this knowledge and gain personal understanding that could closely correspond to the true nature of the elephant.

If this scenario happened, would these men now know everything about the elephant with certainty? No, but they would know enough to live their lives with understanding and a justified belief that the elephant (truth) exists and a great deal of knowledge about what the elephant is like. Because any one man, or collection of men, does not know all truth, this does not in the least change truth or its existence. Because we do not know everything about the elephant does not mean we cannot know some things accurately. It is possible to know a significant amount of truth through personal or shared experience and knowledge, logical thinking, and revelation given by entities that see clearly.

What is sometimes forgotten or ignored is that no one seeks truth in a vacuum.

Truth is defined here as that which conforms to physical, spiritual, and moral reality. In this way, truth does not change for each individual; it is absolute in nature. A person's perception of truth may vary, but the truth does not. The million-dollar question, then, is this: Can a person know if truth exists? Yes, and the wise person will work to gain as much information about truth as possible, so he will know how to live well. After all, truth, much like an elephant, can be a useful friend, or it can trample a person who ignores its presence.

Are There Moral Absolutes?

If a person accepts that knowledge of truth is possible, the next concern is whether or not truth, and in this case, moral truth, does exist. A moral truth, or moral absolute, is something that is true for all people, times, cultures, circumstances, and places. Interestingly, each person has a built-in sense about this. Most people who hear of a child being raped or a friend being murdered have a response that these actions were morally wrong. Even in a situation where a person breaks into a home to steal food to feed a hungry family, the action seems immoral, even if it is coupled with compassion. Many immoral actions occur, but this does not establish that a certain action is always the most immoral action in every given situation. It does illustrate the existence of moral absolutes. This is an important beginning point.

Even more compelling is that, when pressed, individuals behave as if moral absolutes exist.[1] It is rare to find a thoughtful person who denies the existence of right and wrong. Despite this, today, moral relativism is growing in influence. This view holds that morals are determined either by the individual or by the society.[2] A moral relativist has no basis to say that an action is moral or immoral. They can hold an opinion on the matter, but it is no more binding or correct than the opinion of someone who disagrees with them. Therefore, while you may believe it is wrong to torture babies for pleasure, you would have no basis to say that it is wrong for another person to do this (though you may protest that it is illegal). With moral

---

1 There are some sociopaths who apparently feel no compulsion to do what is right and some others who have mental disorders who are unable to distinguish right from wrong. But our recognition of such disorders points to the fact that the general expectation is that it is "normal" to know and follow certain moral guidelines. Even if their view of "right" is skewed, these individuals still have a sense that they should be treated in a certain "right" way.

2 In this discussion, we will be talking about prescriptive relativism not descriptive relativism. Prescriptive relativism says that morals ought to be relative, while descriptive relativism observes that different moral systems exist.

relativism, the best anyone can do is to say, "I think it is wrong *for me* to torture babies." The moment a person suggests no one should be allowed to torture babies for pleasure, they are taking a moral absolute stance. While moral relativism is growing in popularity in academics and pop culture, people cannot live out this perspective. They will revel in moral relativism to give license to their own lifestyle choices but will hold fast to moral absolutes when evaluating the moral choices of others.

A moral relativist must also be aware of the slippery slope they walk upon. If morality is determined by individuals and groups with no ultimate foundation for any binding moral code, then right and wrong are determined by whoever has the power. A family may think arson is morally acceptable, but the law overrides their view by claiming it to be illegal (and every law is a response to a moral position). The outcome of moral relativism[1] is "might makes right," and those with influence cannot only do what they want but can also claim their actions are moral regardless of what they do. The truth is that few people want to live in a world where morality is defined as the will and actions of the powerful or the majority within any given society.

Another difficulty with moral relativism is that any person who works to be a moral reformer is by definition immoral. All moral reformers (for example, Jesus, Gandhi, or Martin Luther King Jr.) assume that some aspect of current society is immoral. But if society or those with power determine what is moral, then anyone who opposes their view would by definition be immoral. Any moral movement from the status quo would be immoral. In a relativistic society, Moses, Schindler, Lincoln, and Wilberforce would be considered moral perverts and dishonored. For most people, this feels counterintuitive.

---

1   **Relativism:** The view that knowledge, truth, and morality are not absolute, but exist in relation to culture, society, or individual preference.

Next, moral relativism is not livable. As mentioned earlier, people are moral absolutists in their evaluation of how the world should be. This comes across when a person says, "You shouldn't judge me." In saying this, they believe they should be treated in a specific way, in this case without judgment. Yet a moral relativist can only put forward this declaration as a matter of opinion. In addition, if another person judges the moral relativist, they have no grounding to say the other person is wrong; moral relativists do not believe anything is always wrong. In contrast, a moral absolutist does have grounding to identify immorality in themselves and others, when it does not line up with moral truth.

The outcome of moral relativism is "might makes right"...

Further complicating the issue is that moral expression without belief in moral absolutes always leads people into isolation. Without a common view of ethics[1] and a common source for why something is ethical, no common ground exists for preferred right living. Today, in households across America, parents are encouraging their teenage children to make good choices: avoid drugs, don't sleep around, work hard in school, etc. While few would question the moral counsel of these parents, if their teenager(s) pressed for a reason they should follow their parents' advice, without absolute truth the parent has only two possible responses: stand on their authority ("Because I said so!") or list the potential consequences of making bad choices. Neither of these options gives the parent and child common ground for what is a moral choice (for example, it is morally wrong to have sex outside of wedlock). Often, the result of a scene like this is that the parent and teenager add another layer of isolation, as the child views the parents as "old-fashioned"

---

1   **Ethics**: The study or discipline of moral right and wrong.

and "killjoys," and the parents see their children as potentially reckless and immoral.[1]

Finally, when a community or nation of people removes moral absolutes, they become a law (or laws) unto themselves, as people will tend to do what is right in their own eyes. This was the lifestyle of ancient Israel during their historically darkest days as a nation ages ago (Judges 21:25). It is a principle of life, perhaps even a moral absolute, that a person cannot live a life of habitual immorality and get away with it. Our world operates with law-like precision at many levels: The sun rises in the east, sets in the west, and there are certain moral laws that, when ignored or violated, will result in negative consequences. We are a deeply isolated people, yet we long for community; we are foolish, yet we should be wise; we are fearful but desire genuine security; we are aimless but desperately seek purpose; and we are depressed, but we long to be happy. We have incrementally unhinged ourselves from moral absolutes – removing the baby (what actually has value) and keeping the dirty bathwater. I hope we will understand sooner rather than later the high cost of dismissing moral absolutes, so we can adjust our course before we live to regret it.[2]

If Moral Absolutes Exist, What Are They?

We have shown that it is reasonable to accept moral absolutes. It is also reasonable to accept that we can achieve a great deal of knowledge about these moral absolutes when we combine the experience and thinking of mankind both presently and from history. For most people the natural question to ask next is, "Whose moral standard do we accept?"

If a person legalistically attempted to live by a list of moral absolutes, they would quickly encounter numerous problems.

---

1   Whitson, "Concept: Pitching the Baby, Keeping the Bathwater."
2   Ibid.

First moral absolutes can seem to come into conflict with each other, as illustrated in several places in the Bible. In such situations, a person has no choice but to subordinate one moral absolute to another (or ignore them both). In the Bible, Rahab chose between saving the lives of the Israelite spies and telling a lie. Honoring life and speaking the truth are both moral absolutes from Scripture, but in this case, honesty was subordinated to honoring life. Later, Rahab was commended for her actions, even though she had lied. In another case, Abraham needed to choose between obeying God and killing his son. He chose to remain obedient to God and intended to kill his son. He was commended by God for this response. Some argue that this conundrum leads to having no moral absolutes.

It is conceivable for any two moral absolutes to come into irresolvable conflict. On what basis, then, should a person choose which to follow and which to subordinate? The answer to this question requires a moral absolute that judges between other moral principles. This absolute must be so encompassing that it covers all morality and is not internally contradictory. All other ethics and moral truth would be derived from and subordinate to it. In the end, only one moral absolute can exist to which all other ethics and moral truth become derivatives and subordinate.

There is a better answer – one that harmonizes with the book written by the seeing person in the illustration of the six blind men and the elephant. The key is to take God (the Seeing One) as the One who sees, and the Bible as the book He wrote to tell the truth.[1] Though this moral system would make sense apart from the Bible, it is fleshed out by biblical teaching.

---

1   It is not possible to present an argument that unequivocally establishes one moral system over another. It is possible to present reasonable arguments that a moral system that is derived from a personal God makes sense and fits the world better as we find it than other systems fit the world. Due to the constraints of this format, we do not have space to compare and contrast reasons for accepting this system over others. We will assume that previous chapters have established a reasonable defense for why we should accept the Bible as a source of truth.

Why should a person receive God as the author for moral truth? First, the natural universe is a masterpiece that seems to point to a preexistent master of great power and intellect. Regardless of a person's view on how the universe began, all agree that there is tremendous design and wondrous complexity in what exists.[1] Physics and astronomy point to a beginning and a fine-tuned universe that suggests design.[2] Philosophy highlights the need for a beginning to all that exists due to the impossibility of an actual infinite amount of time.[3] Quantum mechanics points to something that brings and maintains order out of uncertainty. Mathematics points to an immaterial set of principles that describe and govern the material world. The inclination of human beings to sense something greater than themselves and have an expectation of order also points to the idea that there exists a Creator.

If the Bible is true, a person would expect to find that same perspective woven throughout its pages, and this is what a person will find. The Bible begins with the idea that there is a master Designer-Creator who sustains order out of chaos. That theme permeates the Bible. It clarifies with specifics the fact of this, which we can observe in nature. Everyone must deal with this one foundational fact – there is a sovereign Creator. We call this entity God. *Sovereign* means that one has the right and ability to do whatever one decides to do. God has the right to do as He desires, because He created all other things from nothing. He therefore has the right of ownership. He has the right of the designer to direct and mold all that He formed. His ability to do what He desires is obvious from His

...an expectation of order also points to the idea that there exists a Creator.

---

1   Recommended reading: *Signature in the Cell* by Stephen Meyer is an excellent starting place.
2   Recommended reading: *A Matter of Days* by Hugh Ross addresses this topic.
3   Recommended reading: *The Last Word* by Thomas Nagel.

demonstrated capacity to create this entire universe. There is no power in heaven or on earth that can hinder anything that God determines to do.[1]

Since there was nothing preceding or external to the Creator, the universe was produced totally from the internal being and character of God. Therefore, the masterpiece of creation will reflect something of His character. God's unchanging character is foundational to all that exists. This has implications in the area of moral absolutes, and the Bible indicates that what may be known of God can be seen in the world. One problem with this is that the masterpiece is much like the elephant to the blind men in the poem shared earlier. The Bible, including its account of Jesus, is like the book about the elephant written by the seeing person and given to the blind men. The Bible helps clarify what we sense about God and the world around us.

As a result, searching for moral absolutes in the Bible is warranted. And subsequently, it would seem reasonable to assume the Bible provides a commandment to guide the implementation of all other moral absolutes. This is, in fact, the case. The top moral absolute that governs all others is to love God with all our heart, mind, body, and soul. A second moral absolute is an extension of the first: A person is to show love for God by loving other people, whom He created in His image (Matthew 22:37-40). All other commandments hang on the Great Commandment like ornaments on a Christmas tree,

---

1 A brief note to forestall certain possible objections: One of the rights that is inherent in sovereignty is God's right to delegate His authority and not to use His power. If God could not limit His authority, or if He could not restrict the use of His power, He would not be sovereign. It seems clear, both in Scripture and by observing the universe around us, that God is not the immediate cause of all that occurs. From the Bible, it is clear that there is at least one specific thing that God does not cause, that being temptation (James 1). Causing temptation is one thing He does not do, and this establishes the principle that God is not the immediate cause of all things. If I can find one thing, then it is a matter of determining what else falls into this category. This has implications for free will and the question about why things happen.

in that all other moral absolutes are moral commands for how to love God and love other people.[1]

The Great Commandment highlights the basic purpose of a human being – to live in a manner that brings pleasure to God. When a person loves God, their lifestyle brings God pleasure. The moral absolutes laid out in the Bible are God's directions to help a person live life well and fulfill their purpose.

In the end, moral absolutes only exist when they are based on the moral character of God. A person cannot create a moral absolute; they can only hold a moral opinion.[2] A person who does not know or love God can still act in accord with His character and perform moral actions. Therefore, belief in God is not a prerequisite to live a moral life. The difference is in a person knowing why they should be moral.

God's choices flowing from His character, coupled with His complete knowledge and perfect understanding, would be the correct moral choice in any given circumstance. The moral person is the one who acts in harmony with God's moral character, given the knowledge that they possess of the circumstances. Therefore, an individual is more or less virtuous based upon the extent to which they have reproduced God's character in themselves and can therefore act in harmony with it. We will be judged on whether or not we meet God's glory by reproducing in ourselves and acknowledging His character in any given

---

1   Before one starts throwing out other instructions/commandments as optional or subject to our understanding, we need to remember that all these instructions were given by the God who knows all things, understands all things, created all things, and loves all things. One knows how to love God because He told us how. If one throws out the "footnotes," that person shows that he thinks he knows better than God how to love Him and other people, whom He designed. This is what 1 John 2:4-10 says. One clearly does not know or love God if he thinks he knows better than God how to love God and other people. Love is not what one feels is loving, but what God knows to be loving. For example, one may think that he is loving by condoning/accepting extra-marital sex. In reality, this is not a loving pursuit. It encourages others to violate God's design and because of that fact, it has negative consequences. The law is good when used lawfully in the context of the one Great Commandment. One should love the law because they love God.

2   This reality highlights that as God is increasingly removed from a person's worldview, only moral relativism can fill the void.

situation. This judgment can only be accomplished by the one being who knows my heart and the standard perfectly – God.

Some might object that this makes it too difficult to judge right from wrong. In reality, this emphasizes the axiom that Christianity is a relationship, not a set of rules. Our one pursuit is to know Christ. This relationship allows us to have the wisdom and understanding to act in accord with His character. When one knows the personal God and reproduces His character, he will know what is right in any given circumstance. Our call is to know God, not to know rules. Rules of morality (laws) were not designed for the righteous, those who have the character of God (1 Timothy 1:9). The law was given as a teacher to lead us to Christ that we might be justified by faith. Within that relationship, God can reproduce His moral character in us.

Conclusion

It is reasonable to believe in the existence of moral absolutes. They are logically undeniable, and humans live as if they exist. Ultimately, moral absolutes are rooted in the character of God and are revealed to mankind through the Scriptures. Because moral absolutes are a part of the fabric of creation, man, who is created in the image of God, has and will continue to struggle to deny their existence. All men live with a sense of some moral absolute, whether or not they act in accord with it. In the end, the moral absolute by which all moral creatures will be judged is the character of God. Activities should be evaluated on this same basis. Therefore, it is incumbent upon us to pursue a personal knowledge of and relationship with God as our first priority.

Discussion Questions

- What is your conclusion? Are there moral absolutes?

- What are a few examples of moral absolutes?

- Why is the existence of moral absolutes so important to our individual lives as well as to how we
  function as a nation?

Chapter 5

How Do I Make Moral Decisions?

By Ryan P. Whitson

Alayna stirred from her sleep, not from the familiar smell of coffee brewing in the nearby kitchen, but from the television set blaring down the hall. She grumbled as she slowly rolled out of bed – 6:45 in the morning – *seriously?* Frustrated, she stumbled down the hall. She forgot everything as her eyes hit the television. With a dropped jaw, she watched an airplane crash into a tower of the World Trade Center on live television.

Do you remember where you were on September 11, 2001? Most people do. The scenes of terror from that morning are etched into the minds of many Americans. They serve as a reminder that evil is alive and well in the world. For months after 9/11, the American people mourned the loss of life and gained an unsettling sense of genuine fear, as a nation cried out in unison that the actions of a handful of terrorists were immoral on a horrific scale.

Or were they?

A moral crisis does exist today. On any night of the week, the evening news spews disturbing stories from local communities to global tragedies that cause many to shake their heads and cry out, "What in the world is going on?" This steady diet of rampant immorality throughout culture has caused many to feel angry and skeptical, especially when individuals or institutions claim to be honest. According to Gallup polling, most Americans see their government, media, and even religious leaders as increasingly unethical and, therefore, untrustworthy.[1] Sadly, in the United States, these are important institutions needed to establish and protect the moral compass of the nation.

In addition, immorality seems to be on the rise everywhere in American culture. A recent study of ethics in the workplace revealed that over 56 percent of employees regularly see illegal or unethical conduct at work that violates their company's code of ethics or the law.[2] Ethical problems also exist in higher education. According to the Josephson Institute, 59 percent of high school students plagiarize on writing assignments and tests.[3] Ironically, while immorality appears to be on the rise, most Americans still view themselves as good citizens (97 percent), friendly (94 percent), and generous (90 percent).[4]

But today's moral crisis goes far deeper and gets more confusing, because substantial doubt is increasing that actual morality even exists. It is nothing new or remarkable to have a group of people disagree about what is moral. It is also not a shock to see people (or ourselves) make immoral decisions. But when a society begins to doubt there is such a thing as real right and wrong, the moral crisis goes to a completely new and twisted level.[5]

The confusion begins with the obvious observation. The

---

1   This claim comes from three separate articles in which Gallup polls are cited. Regarding the government, see *abcnews.go.com/blogs/politics/2013/12/congress-bottoms-out-in-new-honesty-and-ethics-ratings/*. Regarding the media, see *www.poynter.org/latest-news/mediawire/233954/still-slip-sliding-gallup-poll-ranks-journalists-low-on-honesty-ethics/*. Regarding clergy, see *www.gallup.com/poll/166298/honesty-ethics-rating-clergy-slides-new-low. aspx*.

2   Jeff Madura, *Introduction to Business* (St. Paul, MN: Paradigm Publishing, 2010), 52.

3   *www.plagiarism.org/resources/facts-and-stats*.

4   *www.breakingchristiannews.com/articles/display_art.html?ID=2895*.

5   The word *morality* is still frequently used. What has changed is the meaning behind the word. Today, for an increasing number of people, it no longer refers to a moral absolute that is universally and objectively true.

same nation that bemoans the rampant immorality around them largely doubts that actual morality exists. This is akin to lamenting feeling hungry and then doubting that food exists. The current ethical dilemma in the United States is twofold: an increase in what most agree is immoral and an increasing doubt that moral truths actually exist.

The increasing doubt today that moral truth exists primarily comes from the rise of postmodernism. This is the worldview of choice among American pop culture and, while this worldview has many facets, its primary philosophical claim is that absolute truth does not exist.[1] The word *truth* still exists and is used often, but what people mean when they use the term is usually much different today from years past. Truth no longer refers to a correct proposition that corresponds to reality in an absolute, universal, and objective way. Today the word *truth* can mean just about anything nonbinding, such as my opinion, perspective, preference, belief, or value.

Yet people live their lives each day as if absolute truth does exist and is useful.

Yet people live their lives each day as if absolute truth does exist and is useful. People use mathematics with confidence to work out their finances and are careful not to drop hammers and bowling balls on their toes, because they believe gravity is true. I could go on and on with examples like this to demonstrate that people live as if there are things in this world that really are true, and a postmodernist would agree – to a point.

Most postmodernists would agree that truth exists in areas such as science and mathematics, because these disciplines have the tools to test truth-claims in empirical and repeatable ways.[2]

---

1   Please notice the hypocrisy of the postmodern claim, "There is no absolute truth." The death of absolute truth also slays the postmodernist claim, and, therefore, should *not* be believed. A postmodernist should not be allowed to accept absolute truth to support their claims, but deny it exists for everyone else.

2   A person can use the scientific method in this process. This does not work well in the humanities.

As a result, a much higher degree of confidence exists that true knowledge can be known about red blood cells and chemical compounds as opposed to moral claims. Therefore, when a person makes the claim, "It is wrong to murder another human being," there may be agreement from others, from the law, and from various religious doctrines, but this collective agreement does not necessarily make the statement true (or false). All that can be asserted is that a particular person or group holds the opinion, belief, or preference that killing another person is morally wrong. For the majority of Americans, the best ethics has to offer are moral suggestions that can help people form their own perspectives, beliefs, and values.

A Christian will most likely find this dilemma perplexing, even disturbing, because the existence of moral truth, a real and binding right and wrong, is based on the character of God and woven into the message of the Bible and human experience. God, who alone has authority to determine what is moral, reveals in Scripture what all people know intuitively and experience daily: There is good and evil in the world.[1] As a result, a Christian can have confidence in *who* determines morality – it is God alone.

Regarding this idea, that morality is rooted in the character of God, skeptics might look to Socrates and his famous question: Is something good because God commands it, or does God command it because it is good?[2] The problem this question poses is this: If something is moral simply because God commanded it, then God could have issued a different command, and therefore right and wrong are arbitrary. Or are some things moral in themselves and independent of God's commands? Whichever way this question is answered, it damages the idea that God is God and the very essence of morality.

---

1   This intuitive sense of right and wrong is also called a person's conscience, which is God's moral law written upon the hearts of all people.

2   This is called the Euthyphro Dilemma.

The dilemma is explained when it is seen that both Old and New Testament morality are grounded in the nature and character of God. Therefore, morality is not a necessary thing independent from God, but it is declared ethical by God because it is rooted in His unchanging character and nature. As an example, murder is evil because God's nature and character is life. Injustice is immoral because God is just. Moral truth is not arbitrary, and God commands moral actions that are rooted in His unchanging nature and character.

While God commands His people to live moral lives, a person does not need to believe in God to be ethical and to do good works in the world. An estimated 90 percent of Americans say they believe in God, but this does not mean that 90 percent of Americans are ethical.[1] A person who is agnostic toward God can still make ethical choices, and a person who believes in God can make unethical decisions. The primary problem for a person who dismisses God as the authority for moral truth is not that they can no longer do moral acts, but that they have a hard time explaining both *who* determines right and wrong and *why* they should do moral deeds. In contrast, a Christian does not have an issue with *who* determines morality or *why* they should do moral deeds.[2] The challenge for a Christian lies in the effort to determine *what* is good and then choosing to do it.

The purpose of this chapter is to address this very challenge: How does a Christian determine what is moral in order to make an ethical decision? This question dismisses the postmodern idea of morality and assumes there is such a thing as moral truth or a moral target that has an actual bulls-eye worth aiming for. If postmodernism explains how the world really is (where there is no moral truth), then it is not worth the time to ask a question about how to make moral decisions. If

---

1   *www.ewtnnews.com/catholic-news/US.php?id=3372.*

2   The reason a Christian should do moral deeds is to honor God with their life. Obedience shows a love for God.

a moral decision is fundamentally doing what *I* think is right and nothing more, then the question is really addressing how a person makes any kind of decision, such as whom to marry or what to order from a fast-food menu. But if moral truth exists and people can discover it and live it out, then learning how to make ethical decisions carries real value.

How to Make Moral Decisions

A big part of the human experience is making decisions. Every day people make choices: when to get up, what to wear, where to go, what to say, and many more. Some choices are routine, almost mindless, while others are significant and difficult. People make choices, and then their choices make them. Some even say a person's life is the sum of their decisions. In light of this, making choices that are moral and avoiding what is evil really does matter. A person who chooses right over evil will notice the benefits in their personal relationships, such as enjoying trust with others. Choosing to be ethical brings a sense of personal satisfaction and inner peace; it allows the individual to avoid guilt and shame. When followers of Jesus align their lives with His commands, fulfillment follows that obedience and the desire to honor God.

People make choices, and then their choices make them.

Morality also matters to all people in the affairs of everyday life. When an individual or community strives to live out what is right and avoid what is evil, people prosper in the areas of politics, relationships, academics, sports, and more. Conversely, an individual or community is harmed when immorality is the norm. Occasions such as the terrorist attacks in America on September 11, 2001, blow away the idea that morality is not important or that there is no moral truth. What is clear is that each person needs the skills to know how to make ethical choices.

Below is a five-step guide to help determine what is moral.[1] The guide may feel clunky because of the number of steps, and cumbersome due to the speed of real-life decision-making. But I believe the flow of these steps can be assimilated and this process can become intuitive and useful. But even if this decision-making guide does not become intuitive, the process still has value as a guide to slow a person down as they make decisions. Most people have experienced making a regretful choice because it was made with haste. This five-step guide will help you think through how to make a moral choice, especially when the ethical issues are perplexing.

Step 1 ⎰ Gather the Facts ⎱

When facing a moral choice, it is important to ask two questions:

1. What do I already know regarding the choice before me?

2. What do I need to know regarding the choice before me?

There is value in taking a few moments or even a few days to go on a fact-finding mission regarding the decision a person is facing. Proverbs 25:7-8 echoes this idea when it instructs: *What you have seen with your eyes do not bring hastily to court, for what will you do in the end if your neighbor puts you to shame?* In other words, a person should form their opinions carefully and be wary of the assumptions they hold before gathering all the facts. Without this, a person may find that what they thought they knew of a situation was inaccurate, that they jumped to a conclusion, or that what they needed to know was different from what they originally thought. Some moral issues create controversies simply because people do not bother to check the facts. Do not overlook this first step. Do not be hasty. Finally,

---

1   For a similar ethical decision-making process, see Scott Rae's book *Moral Choices.*

remember that as a person gathers the information they need to make a moral decision, the facts by themselves only tell a person what is; they do not tell a person what they ought to do. Additional steps in our decision-making guide are necessary.

Step 2 – Determine the Moral Issue(s)

This step addresses the question: What is the moral issue(s) at hand? The ability to respond well to this question depends on whether or not step 1 was completed. Discerning the moral issues associated with a choice requires the formation of a clear picture with all the pertinent facts. As an example, suppose John had a free afternoon to himself and had a choice to either mow his lawn or go bowling with his friends. This decision does not appear to have any moral issues attached. But suppose John had promised his wife he would mow the lawn that afternoon. Gathering this fact helps to see that an ethical issue is at play, namely, whether John will keep his promise and cut the grass.

When determining the ethical issue(s), a person will often lay out their pending decision in these different ways:

"If I do X, the outcome will be …." This approach uses consequences to uncover the moral issues. For example, if John chooses to go bowling and not keep his promise to his wife, he will have lied and broken trust with his wife. This will result in harmful consequences, such as an argument or John's wife being disappointed in her husband. Using this approach, called consequentialism, is tricky, because a bad outcome to an action does not always mean it is unethical, and a good outcome to an action does not always mean it is moral.

"Would person P do X?" This approach holds up an example of a virtuous person to determine how they would choose. This person might be a friend, a relative, Jesus Christ, or any other person someone determines to best exemplify moral living. Using the same scenario, John, as a Christian, might ask the question, "What would Jesus do?" He would determine that Jesus would not break a promise; therefore, John should choose to mow his lawn and keep his word to his wife.

"What does God say about doing X?" A Christian (or anyone, for that matter) does well to go to the Bible to learn God's commands on a variety of moral issues.

There are other ways to think through a moral decision in order to determine the ethical issues, but these examples demonstrate how the process might look. In this step, a person should take the facts of their situation and determine what moral issue(s) are at play.

Step 3 – Determine How You Will Make a Moral Choice

After gathering facts and determining the relevant ethical issue(s), you must determine *how* to make a moral choice. In a sense, you will decide how you will decide.

Every person, whether they realize it or not, uses an approach or principle to make their ethical decisions. The study of ethics provides several types of approaches or theories that people can use and have used to try to do what is right. The key question in this step is, "What ethical theory should I use to best help me make the right decision?" It is suggested here that a follower of Jesus will find three ethical theories most helpful to making decisions that are both morally correct and pleasing to God.

The first and most common approach a Christian will use to make a moral choice is often called the Divine Command

Theory (DCT).[1] This approach uses the commands of Scripture to determine good and evil. In many cases, this approach is clear-cut: If God commands something to be done, it is moral;. if He forbids something from happening, then it is immoral. Thankfully, the Bible has much to say about morality, which can make DCT very helpful. For example, in the Old Testament there are hundreds of commands from God to do certain things (tell the truth, love a neighbor, etc.) and not to do others (commit adultery). The New Testament also provides commands and instruction on moral topics such as justice, politics, and how to treat people. The primary strength of this theory is the clear and timeless direction provided for discerning right and wrong on a variety of topics, which can give a Christian a settled posture, knowing they are doing what pleases God.

This would appear to settle all questions for how a Christian should make a moral choice, but this is unfortunately not the case. Divine Command Theory does have two weaknesses.[2] First, sometimes the Bible does not speak to a specific moral issue. For example, should a Christian airline steward serve liquor to passengers? Should a Christian lawyer represent a guilty client? In other cases, the Bible speaks to a moral issue, but not in a clear manner, such as whether people should keep slaves[3] or women should be forced into marriage.[4] This latter example highlights that some moral commands in the Bible appear to be for a specific time and culture and not applicable to all people for all times; yet discerning which commands are for us is not always easy.

A second weakness of DCT is that God's commands

---

1   This section is writing to Christians, but any person who applies these approaches will find benefit to making moral choices, though likely for different motivations.

2   This does not in any way question the value, inspiration, or need to learn and apply Scripture, but only highlights that there may be times the Divine Command Theory is not sufficient.

3   Leviticus 25:44-46.

4   Deuteronomy 21:10-12.

sometimes come in conflict in a given situation. These situations are rare, but can be highlighted by considering whether one person should tell a lie in order to protect the life of another person. This dilemma faced Christian hero Corrie ten Boom as her family hid Jews from Nazi authorities during World War II. In a biblical example, in Joshua 2:1-4 the prostitute Rahab lied to protect the Israelite spies. It would appear from Hebrews 11:31 and James 2:25 that Rahab's actions were commended, despite her dishonesty. Often, situations where people find the ethical commands of the Bible in conflict arise because of poor reading of the text and violating hermeneutical rules, but the weakness remains regarding DCT.[1]

Despite its weakness, I would argue that DCT holds tremendous value and should be the first approach a Christian should take in knowing what is moral. Taking this step first will be a great help in most ethical dilemmas faced by a person.

A second ethical approach that is helpful to the Christian making a moral choice is called Virtue Ethics. This approach addresses the question, What sort of person should I be? The goal is to be a person of character who demonstrates virtue through thoughtful, habitual actions. In other words, a good person will do good actions. With this theory, to determine what is right or wrong, one need not apply a complex standard of conduct to a decision, its outcome, or the motive of the doer. A good man simply does good works in a habitual way. Virtue Ethics helps a Christian make moral decisions, because it intentionally holds up Jesus Christ as the ideal portrait to be emulated for what is good. Therefore, a Christian should strive to live like Jesus Christ.

A good man simply does good works in a habitual way.

---

1   Hermeneutics is the art and science of interpreting the Bible and, as a subject, has
     Bible reading rules to help a person properly understand what they are reading.

In this way, good is something Jesus would do, say, or think; evil is something He would avoid. This theory partners well with the Divine Command Theory, since Jesus perfectly obeyed the Scriptures, and the commands of the Bible are best exemplified in the sinless life of Christ. Therefore, He is the ideal model of how to live a moral life. This allows a person to prayerfully pursue, with the Holy Spirit's enabling, a life modeled after Jesus with full confidence that they are also living a moral life. Approaching ethics with the example of Jesus Christ in mind is a substantial help for a Christian facing a moral dilemma.

A third ethical approach that can help a Christian make a moral decision is called Deontology.[1] This view focuses on the intentions behind a behavior rather than on the outcome. This ethical theory argues that a person should do some things, even if they result in negative or uncomfortable consequences; likewise, a person should not do other things, even if the outcome is positive. This view has been best promoted by the philosopher Immanuel Kant who developed the Categorical Imperative concept. Although there are various versions of this approach, it is best known in its original version: Act only according to that maxim which can, at the same time, become a universal law.[2]

To illustrate this, consider the question: Should a person steal a candy bar from the local grocery store? This view doesn't rely on a list of dos or don'ts, but rather asks the question: Can I say that every person should be able to do what I am about to do – in this case, steal a candy bar? Clearly, theft should not be endorsed as a universal law; therefore, this individual should not steal the candy. Many have correctly noticed that this approach resembles the Golden Rule, which states, "Treat others how you wish to be treated." This law of reciprocity is found throughout history in various religions and philosophical

---

1   This view is also called nonconsequentialism.
2   Immanuel Kant, *Grounding for the Metaphysics of Morals (Third Edition)*, trans. James W. Ellington (Indianapolis, IN: Hackett Publishing Company, 1993), 30.

movements, as well as with the words of Jesus Christ when He said, *Do to others what you would have them to do to you, for this sums up the Law and the Prophets.*[1] While there is debate as to whether the Categorical Imperative and the Golden Rule are identical or only similar, both still highlight that you should act toward others in ways you would want everyone else to act toward others, yourself included.[2]

One must think carefully about how a decision will impact others. The Categorical Imperative and the Golden Rule both serve as guides for living with love. Doing the right thing is always the goal, but being right without any effort to love can result in cruelty. In contrast, loving others without moral truth can result in hypocrisy. Jesus' example was the perfect blend of grace and truth in how He treated people with love. In fact, in John 1:14 Jesus is described as one who was *full of grace and truth.* He always did what was moral and did it in a loving and gracious manner toward others. Every Christian should pursue this.

Recap

There are a few valuable steps for a Christian trying to determine how to make a moral decision:

Step 1

Go to the Bible to discern what God says about a moral dilemma.

Step 2

Look to the example of Jesus Christ: What would Jesus say or do in this moral dilemma?

---

1   Matthew 7:12; Luke 6:31. The Golden Rule has Old Testament roots in Leviticus 19:18, 34.
2   Kant himself felt the Categorical Imperative was an improvement of the Golden Rule and not an identical idea.

Step 3

How will my decision impact the lives of others and my community around me?

Step 4

List any Alternatives

Before making a decision, take time to make a list of alternative courses of action. It may be difficult, but push yourself to come up with other courses of action you've not yet considered. What are your options? Thinking

Thinking through other options can be helpful in doing what is morally correct...

through other options can be helpful in doing what is morally correct. In addition, talking to and getting advice from others who are trustworthy and spiritually mature is wise. Hearing another point of view will often provide new insight and the right direction.

Step 5

Make a Decision

At some point, a decision needs to be made. It is important to realize that this five-step method does not provide an automatic solution for all moral choices nor does it guarantee the right decision will be made. This method is meant to help identify most of the important ethical considerations.

Making Moral Choices Takes Courage

Several years ago my wife and I found out we were going to have a baby – our fourth! We were excited for this news and greatly anticipated getting to know and hold our new little one. At about the twentieth week of the pregnancy, we picked a date to have the first ultrasound done to get a glimpse of our baby and find out the gender. In our excitement, we pulled the older kids out of school and together made our way to the appointment. As we huddled into the small, dark room, we smiled as we saw our baby, saw her move, and found out it was a little girl.

Then everything went wrong. The ultrasound tech quickly left the room without a word and returned a few minutes later with a doctor. They both silently worked the ultrasound machine. When I asked if everything was okay, they did not respond. Finally, they stopped, turned off the machine, and flipped on the room lights. The show was over and so was our joy. The doctor informed us that our daughter had a condition called anencephaly and she was not going to live. His recommendation was to immediately contact our primary care doctor and schedule an induction. We made this phone call, but requested to take the weekend to talk, think, cry, and pray.

This scenario was personally heart-rending, and we spent most of the weekend in deep grief and shock. But we also had some decisions to make, most immediately and pressing was whether to go through with the induction. We searched online and began reading everything we could find about anencephaly. Most of what we read was difficult and gave us little reason for hope that our girl, barring a miracle, would live more than a few minutes or hours after her birth. As we gathered facts, the cold reality slapped hard that Emily (the eventual name of our daughter) was going to die; there was no intervention or cure for her situation. Her Maker would decide whether she would live or not, and our role was to adjust to this new reality, though we certainly continued to pray for a miracle.

The first dilemma facing us was whether to induce Emily's birth to terminate the pregnancy. As a Christian couple, we wrestled with whether it was morally acceptable to end a life, even if our baby's life span was extremely limited. While some people around us compared this to an abortion scenario, we knew there were differences – we wanted our baby, and at this stage, Laura was in no danger. An induction would simply speed up the inevitable. As we processed the information, we knew God is for life and He decides to give life and take it away.[1] But what if there was a time when Laura was in danger? We considered what Jesus would do in our situation and how our response would impact other people, namely, Emily, Laura, and our family. We slept very little over the forty-eight-hour weekend as we considered any and every option, sought advice, and prayed.

Before the weekend came to a close, we had made a decision we believed was moral and appropriate for the difficult situation we were in.[2] The five-step, decision-making guide, though not sequentially walked through that weekend in our grief, did provide the steps needed to coach us through the issues we were facing. While most of the decisions we face in life are not this emotional, some are just as perplexing and difficult to make.

Conclusion

The key for a Christian who longs to do what is right is the firm belief that moral truth exists, that God is the moral truth-giver, and that making moral choices matters. In addition, seeking God and striving to make a moral decision can take courage, but striving to honor God is always worth the effort. This approach to living brings the most glory to God and the most satisfaction to His people.

---

1   Psalm 139:13-16; Romans 14:8-9.
2   What did we decide to do? To learn more you can read the rest of the story at *emilyjeanstory.blogspot.com*.

Discussion Questions

- What is a moral dilemma you have faced recently (or are facing today)? How did you decide (or how are you deciding) what to do?

- What impact do you see postmodernism is having on morality in our nation?

- This chapter offered a five-step guide to making ethical decisions. In order to practice, apply this approach to an ethical decision you are facing today. What did you learn?

- A Christian will struggle to make moral choices that honor God if they are not spending consistent time reading the Bible. How is this spiritual discipline going in your life today? What is God teaching you from Scripture?

Chapter 6

What Is a Worldview and Why Does It Matter?

By John Hopper

For a while I lived in an area of Houston called Memorial. Memorial is a neighborhood of large, million-dollar houses that are home to some of the city's wealthiest locals. The neighborhood is connected to downtown Houston where many of Memorial's residents work, but in all my years of living in this area, I rarely saw any of the residents take the bus. Why is that? Some may suggest they value independence, efficiency of time, or the status that comes with driving a luxury car. These reasons may be true, but I doubt that when Memorial residents jump in their car instead of hop on the bus, any of these reasons cross their mind. In fact, I would suggest Memorial residents do not struggle over the decision at all, because they have *already* made the decision to take their private car, based on a host of underlying assumptions they are not even aware of.

Every individual holds a set of deep-rooted views that shape the way he or she sees the world. These deep-rooted beliefs are often referred to as a person's *worldview*. A person's values, actions, and choices, such as the transportation they use, the jobs they pursue, and the candidates they elect are all guided by their worldview. Worldviews provide answers to the big questions of life such as:

> When it comes to the natural and supernatural, what is real and how do we know it is real?

> What are the greatest problems facing humanity and how should they be solved?

> Is there such a thing as right and wrong, and, if so, how can we distinguish between the two?

Most people living in the West, including the United States, have a worldview that falls into one of three camps: naturalism, postmodernism, or theism.[1] Understanding how people with these respective worldviews answer questions like those posed above will give us insight into why people think and behave the way they do.

This chapter has two aims. First, I want to provide a brief explanation of naturalism, postmodernism, and theism, so you will have a basic grasp of each way of thinking. Specifically, I will explain each worldview by examining their responses to key topics. My second goal is to present contributions and shortcomings of each worldview to help Christians know how to respond to those who hold a worldview different from their own.

Naturalism

What Is Real?

If someone were to ask you what is real and what is not, you might answer with something like, "The tree in my front yard is real, but the three-headed goblin I saw in the movie last night is not." Naturalists would agree, because naturalism[2] believes

---

1   There are certainly other worldviews, such as animism, deism, or polytheism, but since postmodernism, naturalism, and theism are the more common worldviews in the western world, they are addressed here.

2   **Natural Theology**: Theology or knowledge of God based on observed facts and

reality consists of only what can be found in nature. Reality for the naturalist includes everything on the periodic table and everything those elements combine to make, from water to air or from living creatures to faraway planets. It also includes natural laws like gravity and the second law of thermodynamics.

Naturalism not only states that nature is all there is, but it also holds that science is the key to understanding nature. It is science that identifies the natural elements, which make up the galaxy, the earth we live on, and all living things; and it is science that confirms the laws governing everything from planetary motion to biological development. For the naturalist, science is the only reliable tool for telling us what is real in the world. Wilfred Sellers, an American philosopher and naturalist, echoed this sentiment when he wrote, "In the dimension of describing and explaining the world, science is the measure of all things, of what is that it is, and of what is not that it is not."[1]

> ...it is important to understand that for the naturalist, nature is all there is.

The Natural and the Supernatural

At first glance, naturalism seems like a reasonable worldview. But it is important to understand that for the naturalist, *nature is all there is.* There is no supernatural world. There is no God, no human soul, no abstract objects, nor anything else non-physical. In other words, naturalism is not just espousing scientific knowledge of the natural world; it is also saying the natural world is the only world we can have any knowledge of and that science is the only means to arrive at that knowledge.

---

experience apart from divine revelation.

1   Wilfred Sellers, *Science, Perception and Reality* (New York: Humanities Press, 1963), 173.

Humanity's Greatest Problems

According to naturalists, humans are nothing more than complex combinations of matter. As a result, it is inevitable that naturalists point to the things that threaten our material existence – disease, natural disasters, food shortages, or toxic waste – as humanity's greatest problems. But the obvious natural enemies of our physical well-being are not the only problems that interest naturalists. Those who bully others or steal from a neighbor need to be confronted as well. Rather than turning to spiritual reasons or calling for people to live up to ancient moral codes to fix these disruptive behaviors, naturalists call on science to figure out how to make humans respond better. For example, soon after the 1999 Columbine tragedy in which two high school students killed twelve of their classmates and one teacher, *Newsweek* magazine ran a cover article titled, "Why the Young Kill" that examined biological and sociological factors as the cause of teen violence. In other words, from the perspective of the article's authors, science is the means to correct the shortcomings of our human frailties.[1]

Right and Wrong

When it comes to how we should live, naturalists do not appeal to any religious code or religiously based ethic. Since they do not believe in the supernatural, they do not think people are obligated to abide by any moral behavior found in a holy book or some supernatural source. For the naturalist, there are simply no transcendent morals that tell anyone what is right or wrong. This does not mean they do not recognize right or wrong behaviors. It means that if they do recognize them and if they are consistent with their worldview, right behaviors are ones that allow for their survival and physical health. Furthermore,

---

1   Sharon Begley, Adam Rogers, Pat Wingert, and Thomas Hayden, "Why The Young Kill," *Newsweek*, Vol. 133, No. 18 (May 3, 1999): 32-35.

naturalists often argue that today's moral codes are simply part of our evolutionary development or are a passing socio-biological phenomenon. People who do not kill each other (because their DNA is "bent less towards killing") are more likely to survive than those with the killer instinct.[1] Because morals are just an evolutionary development for the naturalist, they are subject to change and may change even in our day.

Naturalist Worldview Summary

Reality	Natural/ Supernatural	Humanity's Problem	Morality
The material universe is all that exists.	Nature is all there is. There is no supernatural world.	Anything that threatens our material existence is a problem for mankind.	Moral actions support physical health and survivability. There are no moral absolutes.

Naturalism: A Thoughtful Christian's Response

Christians are often quick to address the shortcomings of worldviews different from their own, but first I believe it is valuable to consider positive contributions a different worldview might offer. Naturalism promotes reason and elevates the role of science for attaining knowledge. A Christian should view this as a valuable contribution to learning about the world we all live in. God has placed His fingerprints throughout His creation, often called general revelation, and finding the various reasons to worship Him is the great privilege of humanity. When a person applies their mind to use reason and gains knowledge

---

1   See Robert Wright, *The Moral Animal: Why We Are, the Way We Are: The New Science of Evolutionary Psychology* (Vintage, 1995) for a look at how naturalists explain morality as an evolutionary adaptation.

regarding the natural world, there is a tremendous opportunity to promote God's existence and character.

Secondly, naturalism takes seriously many problems that face humanity, such as disease or natural disaster. This too is a positive contribution of naturalism and is not out of line with the Bible's concern for the sick or those impacted by famine and other natural disasters. The Christian can agree with the naturalist when it comes to the use of reason and science in confronting the physical hardships that are experienced in a fallen world.

...science is making a philosophical claim that only science provides knowledge...

Despite these positive elements, naturalism has several critical shortcomings. The most obvious is that God is left entirely out of the picture. Undoubtedly, this is a problem for the Christian, and for that reason alone, naturalism should be severely questioned. But the Christian can respond to naturalism by doing more than declaring, "But I believe God exists!" He can criticize naturalism based on its own merits.

First, the naturalist claim that knowledge can only be achieved through science is a claim that science itself cannot substantiate. Can a scientist put this claim in a test tube and run a repeatable experiment? Can this claim be put through the scientific method? Of course not. In this instance, science is making a philosophical claim that only science provides knowledge; therefore, the claim fails by its use of philosophy (nonscience) to promote science.

Secondly, discounting the reality of the supernatural based on a tool – the scientific method – that is specifically designed to investigate nature is not legitimate. That would be like a beachcomber declaring the absence of oil under the sand because his metal detector did not reveal the existence of oil. The scientific method is useful to the natural sciences, but this alone does not necessarily mean the supernatural world does not exist.

Third, although one may applaud the use of reason to arrive at knowledge, the reason upon which naturalists rely is suspect. Naturalists believe all of life evolved from the basic elements without divine intervention.[1] This means the brain we have today and the thoughts and reason flowing from it are in a passing evolutionary state. One would then wonder how we can have any confidence that rational thoughts can be generated from an ever-evolving brain. Should we not conclude that what we count as reasonable today will not be reasonable tomorrow for the very reason that our brains will continue to evolve? C. S. Lewis addressed this issue pointedly:

> Supposing there was no intelligence behind the universe, no creative mind. In that case, nobody designed my brain for the purpose of thinking. It is merely that when the atoms inside my skull happen, for physical or chemical reasons, to arrange themselves in a certain way, this gives me, as a by-product, the sensation I call thought. But, if so, how can I trust my own thinking to be true? . . . But if I can't trust my own thinking, of course I can't trust the arguments leading to Atheism [or naturalism], and therefore have no reason to be an Atheist, or anything else.[2]

Fourth, naturalism requires certain rational conclusions to be considered as nothing more than illusions. For example, according to naturalism, humans do not have free choice and, as a result, do not genuinely choose to love; such "states" are simply the result of predetermined biological matter responding

---

1   This view is known as Darwin's macroevolution.
2   C. S. Lewis, *The Case for Christianity* (New York: Macmillan, 1943), 32. *The Case for Christianity* later became the opening chapters of *Mere Christianity*.

to the environment. From my perspective, this does not match up with what people observe. People do have a strong sense that choices are deliberately made and love is freely chosen or avoided. We do not need to doubt these senses any more than one doubts the senses of touch, taste, or smell.

Knowing these shortcomings of naturalism can be helpful to the Christian. For many, the first step to a new worldview is recognizing the inability of one's current worldview to provide a coherent explanation of the world. If a naturalist says there is no God, and the Christian's only response is to say, "Yes, there is a God," they are unlikely to find common ground or agreement. If, however, the naturalist begins to doubt their position, there is an opportunity to consider whether another option, such as Christian theism, is more plausible.

Postmodernism

What Is Real?

Naturalists are quite certain about what is real and how we determine what is real. This is not the perspective of postmodernism.[1] As far as postmodernism is concerned, our pursuit of truth is biased by our upbringing and culture. For example, people in Western cultures often think of science as an objective source of knowledge because of the emphasis on science. But postmodernists question who is able to say that science is a more legitimate source of knowledge than soul travel or shamanism. Thus, when women in tribal cultures are taught that diseases can be prevented through simple acts like the washing of hands, they are justified in looking to the appeasement of local spirits and rejecting Western hygiene practices. In

---

1 One of the first questions asked about the postmodern worldview is, Why is it called postmodernism? The answer to this question comes through an understanding of modernism. Modernism holds the idea that we can attain certainty about knowledge and use that knowledge to create a better world. Because postmodernists reject the certainty espoused by modernity, they consider themselves *postmodern*.

postmodern thought, each person, or at least each culture, has their own truth, and none of their own truth is objectively true.

The Natural and the Supernatural

If each culture creates its own rubric for truth, then all knowledge is subjective. For one culture, Orthodox Judaism is truth; for another, Tibetan Buddhism is truth; and for still another, atheism is truth. Because humans are products of their own culture, they cannot see outside what their culture deems to be true. Perhaps you have heard the words, "You have your truth and I have my truth." These words come from a postmodern perspective. Note that such a perspective does not deny the supernatural; it just says nothing objective can be said about the supernatural, or even the natural.

Humanity's Greatest Problems

As we have seen, postmodernists believe we are trapped in our perspective of the world by the cultural influences around us, and we cannot see objectively. They hold to this tenet so strongly that they see people's claims of objectivity as humanity's greatest problem. Take, for example, the efforts of the Nazis to declare the Arian race superior to all others. In making this claim, Nazis appealed to what they considered objective reasons for their conclusions and destroyed those who rejected them. Had the Nazis simply kept their beliefs to themselves, the destruction of World War II would have been avoided. In looking at this time in history, postmodernism says that the "truth" of Nazism should not have been universalized and was little more than a tool of power for Hitler. Similarly, postmodernism declares that those who argue the objective truth of Christianity or Islam, capitalism or communism, or marriage or free love are not only wrong in making their case, but are also only doing so to control others. If we would all quit trying to convince others we are right about truth, says the postmodernist, peaceful coexistence would ensue, and the world would be a better place to live in. Perhaps you have heard people trumpeting the importance of tolerance at your workplace or school. Such a call for tolerance is at the center of postmodernists' solution to the main struggles they say plague humanity.

Right and Wrong

Postmodernists believe there is no universal truth, at least none that can be known. So when it comes to what is right and wrong, the postmodern person is unable to point to any transcendent ideal people should follow. Instead, the postmodern person says each culture or individual constructs their own ideas of what is right and wrong. In other words, while right and wrong can be identified within a cultural context, they can never be extended beyond a particular culture or ideology. Ironically, postmodernists are quite adamant in saying no universal moral truths exist, but they are known to say it is immoral for a person to say they have discovered objective, universal truth or to be intolerant of what other people believe.

Postmodernist Worldview Summary

Reality	Natural/ Supernatural	Humanity's Problem	Morality
Each person or culture creates their own personal truth. There is no objective truth.	All knowledge is subjective. A person can never truly know about the natural or supernatural world.	Anyone who claims to have objective truth is immoral.	There are no moral truths, but only what an individual or culture collectively agrees is right or wrong.

Postmodernism: A Thinking Christian's Response

Postmodernism has also made a positive contribution to Western-culture worldviews. For example, it highlights the power of culture to shape a person's worldview. A follower of Jesus should be careful that the truth they declare is not merely a collective expression of faith, but is based on what the Bible says is true for people of all cultures. Also, postmodernism provides a healthy warning that some people use "truth" to gain and maintain power over others. History and current politics provide plenty of examples of this occurring, including Marxist communism, the Hindu caste system, or the call for segregation in the southern United States. The Bible itself illustrates the Pharisees using "truth" in an effort to maintain their power.[1] Since the Christian should agree that declarations of truth can be misused for personal gain, they should guard against such a use of truth, but use it for the sake of consistency with the work and Word of God.

...they are saying that it is universally true that you cannot know truth.

Despite these positive contributions, the Christian needs to be aware of several serious philosophical flaws with postmodernism. The primary flaw is postmodernism's declaration that absolute truth does not exist. Postmodernism says a person cannot know universal truth. In making this claim, however, postmodernists are proposing a universal truth; they are saying that it is universally true that you cannot know truth. This sets up their central tenet as self-defeating. At the very best, logically consistent postmodernists can only declare, "I don't know what is true. I don't even know if postmodernism is true." Of course, such a position does not give one much reason to trust in postmodernism.

Since postmodernism is logically self-defeating, postmodernists

---

1   Matthew 23:2-4; 26:62-68; Mark 7:1-13.

have a difficult time living by its tenets in their day-to-day lives. In other words, while postmodernists like to make all "truth" relative, they often behave as if some things are really true. For example, suppose your postmodern friend loves pets, and you tell her you like to carry out experiments on animals (such as holding puppies under water to see how long they take to drown). In no time at all, she will likely tell you that you are wrong to treat animals this way. You might respond by saying, "But I have a different truth about the treatment of animals, and my truth is as valid as yours." I doubt she will accept your objection, because while she might say there are no universal truths, she will act as if some things are always true.

A Christian cannot accept the idea that there is no absolute truth. To accept postmodernism would mean that Christianity is simply a historical collection of opinions held by those under its influence and nothing more. But this is sharply at odds with the Bible's claim that we can know what is true. Take, for example, the words written by the apostle Paul to his younger coworker Timothy: *I urge that requests, prayers, intercessions, and thanks be offered on behalf of all people .... Such prayer for all is good and welcomed before God our Savior, since **he wants all people to be saved and to come to a knowledge of the truth*** (1 Timothy 2:1-4 NET, emphasis added). According to this passage, the message of Christ is not just knowledge for a Christian subset of people; it is for all people. This is certainly not consistent with postmodern thinking and should give Christians reason to be suspicious regarding postmodernism.

Another critique of postmodernism, as we have seen in earlier chapters, brings to light that it has great difficulty supporting reform within a culture. To consider improving culture requires the view that the culture is not as it should be; this, however, is a truth-claim. Without absolute truth, we have no hope of reforming social evils like racial and gender inequality.

A final critique of postmodernism illustrates that its mantra of tolerance is not quite as tolerant as it sounds. Postmodernism gives each person the freedom to create their own ideas of truth. As a result, every idea must be tolerated by every person. However, at least one exception exists: Postmodernists are quite intolerant of those who hold to the existence of absolute truth. The result is that postmodernists are accepting of other postmodernists, but a Christian will be viewed as intolerant, bigoted, and even dangerous.

Theism

Naturalism and postmodernism are certainly prevalent in Western culture. Most likely as you read the above descriptions, people came to mind who embrace one of those two worldviews. Theism, however, has the deepest roots in Western culture and is still very alive today. Practicing Christians, Jews, and Muslims hold this worldview. As with naturalism and postmodernism, we shall define theism and then discuss some criticisms and strengths.

What Is Real?

Theists believe people can know and understand things through reason (like naturalists) and culture (like postmodernists), but theists also believe that knowledge can come from divine revelation. This revelation may be attained through a variety of means, including dreams and visitations, but perhaps most importantly it is received through written revelation. For the Jew, this written revelation is the Old Testament; for the Christian, it is the complete Bible (Old and New Testaments); and for the Muslim, it is the Qur'an. Because the theist recognizes limits to human reasoning and the existence of cultural biases, greatest weight is always given to divine revelation. In the end, theists believe God is responsible for any accurate assessment of reality humans possess. God accomplishes this through the reason He has granted, the cultures that have been shaped by His ways, and the divine revelation which He made directly accessible.

The Natural and the Supernatural

Naturalism says that reality is only made up of matter, and postmodernism says that reality is determined by culture and is relative. Theism, on the other hand, says that reality is made up of both the material and the immaterial. Further, it argues that the two interact with one another, and truth about both can be known. More specifically, theists believe a supreme supernatural being (God) interacts with humanity in history. They also believe that humans are made of both biological material and an immaterial soul.

Humanity's Greatest Problems

Theists recognize, as do naturalists, that humanity faces great natural challenges. Diseases, environmental factors, and physical quality-of-life issues are problems for peoples of all races, gender, and socio-economic status. Theists also recognize, as do postmodernists, that humanity's culturally biased perspective and those who are intolerant of different opinions pose challenges. But theists do not see these concerns as the greatest problems for humanity. The fundamental human problem for the theist is how people respond to God, His design for the world, and His pattern for a flourishing life.

Theists hold that God is the Supreme Being in the cosmos and is worthy of worship and obedience. They also hold that God created the world and has the best understanding of how people should live. When humans choose not to recognize God as the rightful ruler and do not live in the way that He has revealed we should live, people do not get along well with others, fall prey to addictions, and take pathways destructive to both themselves and others. For example, a theist would say that when a husband regularly beats his wife, he does not do so because his DNA makes him or because of cultural influences, but rather because he has not responded correctly to God's ways.

Another problem for humanity from a theistic perspective is the influence of evil supernatural powers in the world. While some theists only believe in good super- natural forces, many hold to the traditional position that evil supernatural beings exist as attested to in the Old and New Testaments and

Humanity has more than proven it is incapable of living up to God's standard...

in the Qur'an. These evil beings, while not holding complete sway over humanity, can influence people away from God and cause considerable hardship.

Finally, when considering the problems facing humanity, many theists believe that a person's rejection of God and His ways, as encouraged by supernatural evil powers, not only creates problems in the present, but also affects the individual's eternal destiny. Notice the following words by Jesus in the book of Matthew:

> *This is how it will be at the end of the age. The angels will come and separate the wicked from the righteous and throw them into the blazing furnace, where there will be weeping and gnashing of teeth.* (Matthew 13:49-50)

What is the theist's solution to this terrible plight? Many theists believe salvation is achieved through a sincere pursuit of good works in accordance with God's revealed ways. For these theists, if a woman's good acts outweigh her bad and she is sincere in her effort to live right before God, she will escape damnation at death. For the Christian theist, however, salvation cannot be achieved through self-effort. Humanity has more than proven it is incapable of living up to God's standard. The Christian theist believes humanity needs the undeserved forgiveness of God made possible through Jesus Christ, who paid the penalty by His death for our rebellious ways. With this in mind, the Christian theist contends that if we respond to Jesus by acknowledging that His sacrifice on our behalf and His authority over our lives is the only hope, then we are granted the privilege of living with God forever.

Right and Wrong

For both naturalism and postmodernism, no universal or time-enduring morals exist. People may choose to enforce or encourage certain types of behavior because they help us physically or because they help people within our culture operate in some cohesive manner. Theism does not take this stance. Instead, God has the right to declare what is right and wrong, and our responsibility is to live out what is right in His eyes.

Most theists will say that certain actions like murder or adultery are against the will of God. But beyond specific dos or don'ts, Christian theists point to the character of God in Scripture as being prescriptive for human behavior. For example, God describes Himself as *the compassionate and gracious God, slow to anger, abounding in love and faithfulness, maintaining love to thousands, and forgiving wickedness, rebellion and sin. Yet he does not leave the guilty unpunished.*[1] As those under God's rule, Christian theists believe they are to imitate such characteristics.

---

1   Exodus 34:6-7.

Theistic Worldview Summary

Reality	Natural/ Supernatural	Humanity's Problem	Morality
God exists; He created the material world. Reality is both material and spiritual.	Both the natural and supernatural world exist.	Mankind's rebellion from God into sin presents our dilemma.	Morality is objective because it is grounded in God's unchanging character.

Theism: A Thinking Christian's Response

Over the centuries, criticisms of the theistic worldview have arisen. For example, the existence of suffering, the plurality of religions, and the apparent uselessness of God due to the advances of modern science are a few of the attacks on theism. Each of these topics, and several others, will be addressed in other chapters in this book. For now, my preference is to provide a few positive reasons for preferring theism (and particularly Christian theism) over the other two worldviews.

First, reason within the theistic worldview is not self-defeating. Reason cannot be trusted with naturalism or postmodernism, because thinking is either a passing evolutionary state or a temporal cultural construction. Theism, on the other hand, assumes reason as a timeless God-given gift, which makes it a rational basis for belief.

Second, theism fits with the design seen in the world. Whereas naturalism has to explain away the appearance of design in the universe, theism easily explains this appearance by appealing to an intelligent designer.[1] Theists not only point

---

1   The universe has so many marks of design, it compelled Frances Crick, a co-discoverer of DNA and a nontheist, to say, "Biologists must constantly keep in mind that what they see was not designed, but rather evolved." Francis Crick, *What Mad Pursuit: A Personal View of Scientific Discovery* (New York: Basic Books, 1990), 138.

to divine revelation, but they also present a rational verdict for the appearance of design found in the cosmos from DNA coding to the expansion of the universe.[1]

Third, unlike postmodernism, theism allows for individuals and cultures to be reformed without the use of power or environmental manipulation. As mentioned earlier, postmodernism provides no basis for social reformation, and naturalism gives no grounds for the dignity of human life (we are nothing but collections of matter). Theism, however, allows people to draw on transcendent God-given values like justice and mercy to anchor protests against those who seek to belittle and harm any segment of humanity.

Fourth, theism provides a basis for morality, love, and beauty. If a naturalist says they love a child, a painting is beautiful, or a rapist is bad, they are only saying they are having a chemical reaction towards the objects. In the same situation, the postmodernist is saying they are having a cultural response that they cannot control. These responses are not the reality by which people intuitively live.

These responses are not the reality by which people intuitively live.

Finally, theism provides an attainable and straightforward solution to the problem of evil and destruction in the world that is available to people in every culture, regardless of their access to scientific information. This is especially true of Christian theism, which holds that people in every age and location can turn to God and receive His mercy and grace as well as find the power and direction to live a more virtuous life. Furthermore, the Christian theist can have hope in the midst of pain and suffering, knowing that a balance of justice will come in the life to come.

---

1   For more on how the appearance of design points to an intelligent Creator, see *The Case for a Creator* by Lee Strobel and *Intelligent Design: Uncensored* by William A. Dembski and Jonathan Witt.

Conclusion

This brief explanation and critique of naturalism, postmodernism, and theism is sufficient to recognize each as a fundamentally different way of viewing the world. We can see that these different worldviews can and do substantially impact the way people think and behave. While there are positive aspects to naturalism and postmodernism as rational worldviews, I believe they have less validity than a theistic worldview. Many Christians believe that people must simply take Christianity by faith, but this faith need not be devoid of reason. There are good reasons to reject naturalism and postmodernism, and there are good reasons to embrace theism as a coherent worldview.

Discussion Questions

- Can you identify people who fit into each of the three worldview categories? What have they said that makes you think they fall in one worldview camp or another?

- Which of the arguments against naturalism or postmodernism was most compelling?

- What might be the advantage of acknowledging the positive contributions of a worldview with which you don't agree?

- How might a person's worldview impact their perspective on current social and political issues? For conversation sake, select a few topics of interest to discuss.

Chapter 7

Do All Religions Teach the Same Thing?

By Darrell Dooyema

I am the way and the truth and the life. No one comes to the Father except through me. —Jesus

"God can be realized through all paths. All religions are true. The important thing is to reach the roof. You can reach it by stone stairs or by wooden stairs or by bamboo steps or by a rope. You can also climb up by a bamboo pole."
—Sri Ramakrishna

Have you ever heard the idea that there are many paths to God? Or that perhaps all religions are essentially saying the same thing using different words? Could the Muslim idea of Allah, the Hindu idea of Vishnu, the Buddhist idea of Brahman, and the Christian idea of God be the same person described with different terms? Does Jesus sound a bit snobbish or exclusive when He claims He is the only way to God? A Buddhist professor recently remarked to me, "It's not so much that we differ in belief; it is more that we just have different practices."

Could he be right that each religion merely employs a different approach to accessing God? When the Muslim bows five times a day to pray, or a Hindu engages in Hatha yoga, or a Buddhist spends time in meditation, are they really doing the same thing as a Christian who seeks God in prayer?

Ironically, my professor friend might very well have had it exactly backwards. G. K. Chesterton responds to the idea that religions are similar in belief yet different in practice like this: "It is false; it is the opposite of the fact. The religions of the earth do not greatly differ in rites and forms; they do greatly differ in what they teach."[1] In other words, just as a green apple and a tennis ball may look similar on the outside, with one bite we can discover that they certainly have a different core. People from many religions celebrate religious holidays, attend group meetings, practice prayer or meditation, and view charity as a good work. Yet these surface-level similarities are motivated by very different ideas about God, humanity, salvation, and our eternal destination. What is more, these different teachings are not complimentary but are contradictory. In fact, all religions make exclusive claims, and these contradictory claims cannot all be true. Instead of climbing to the same destination using different routes, the religious people of the world are climbing toward different destinations.

In this chapter, we will explore some of these major differences. We will discover that world religions differ greatly in their view of God or ultimate reality, their view of humanity, their idea of salvation, and their idea of eternal destination. Those who wish to claim that all religions teach the same thing take an overly simplistic view of religion in general and end up disrespecting other religions. Finally, we will consider the exclusive claims of Jesus and ask what the implications of His statements may be.

---

1   G. K. Chesterton, "The Romance of Orthodoxy," *Page by Page Books*: www.pagebypage-books.com/Gilbert_K_Chesterton/Orthodoxy/The_Romance_of_Orthodoxy_p4.html (July 6, 2015).

The Blind Men and the Elephant

An old story attempts to argue for the idea that all religions are merely different ways of explaining or interpreting the world.[1] It claims to show that there is not one explanation, but multiple interpretations. The poem below describes the story:

> It was six men of Indostan,
>   To learning much inclined,
> Who went to see the Elephant
>   (Though all of them were blind),
> That each by observation
>   Might satisfy his mind.
>
> The First approached the Elephant,
>   And happening to fall
> Against his broad and sturdy side,
>   At once began to bawl:
> "God bless me! but the Elephant
>   Is very like a wall!"
>
> The Second, feeling of the tusk,
>   Cried, "Ho! What have we here
> So very round and smooth and sharp?
>   To me 'tis mighty clear,
> This wonder of an Elephant
>   Is very like a spear!"
>
> The Third approached the animal,
>   And happening to take
> The squirming trunk within his hands,
>   Thus boldly up and spake:
> "I see," quote he, "the Elephant
>   Is very like a snake!"

---

1   This same parable was referred to in chapter 4 on moral absolutes.

The Fourth reached out an eager hand,
And felt about the knee:
"What most this wondrous beast is like
Is mighty plain," quoth he:
"'Tis clear enough the Elephant
Is very like a tree!"

The Fifth, who chanced to touch the ear,
Said: "Even the blindest man
Can tell what this resembles most;
Deny the fact who can,
This marvel of an Elephant
Is very like a fan!"

The Sixth no sooner had begun
About the beast to grope,
Then, seizing on the swinging tail
That fell within his scope,
"I see," quoth he, "the Elephant
Is very like a rope!"

And so these men of Indostan
Disputed loud and long,
Each in his own opinion
Exceeding stiff and strong,
Though each was partly in the right,
And all were in the wrong![1]

Does this humorous poem prove that all religions essentially teach the same thing or that objective truth is not possible? Actually, it proves the opposite, but we need to investigate to discover why.

In order for the story to make sense, there must be only one

---

1   Saxe, "The Blind Men and the Elephant," *www.allaboutphilosophy.org/blind-men-and-the-elephant.htm.*

real and objective truth – a real elephant! The existence of the truth (the real elephant) gives the story its whole point. Thus, the story cannot illustrate the idea of relativism – that objective truth does not exist or is forever hidden behind endless interpretations. Neither does it illustrate the idea that we can all be right about our interpretation of God. The three blind men who felt parts of the elephant were not all correct in their understanding. Instead, they were all wrong, describing merely an attribute of the elephant rather than understanding what an elephant really is. What is more, in order for the story to be told at all, someone who understands why these optically challenged explorers respond as they do must be observing the real elephant. The narrator of the story *makes an exclusive claim* to know this real and objective truth. The elephant story merely illustrates that people can misunderstand the truth about the world.

...there must be only one real and objective truth – a real elephant!

Different religions also make different claims about the truth of the world.

In the elephant story, each of the blind men offered an aspect of the elephant as a simile: "The elephant is *like* a wall" or "The elephant is *like* a spear." When seen from the perspective of the narrator, all these similes fit together. But this is not what different religions teach about reality. Instead of describing different aspects of God that could fit together, they offer contradictory claims about the nature of God and the nature of reality. To claim someone is "skinny like a string bean" is very different from claiming that someone *is* a string bean. Rather than merely offering compatible ideas of what God is *like*, religions actually offer contradictory ideas about the essential nature and identity of God.

When considering contradictory claims, one must be true

and the other false. Basic laws of logic teach us the same. The law of non-contradiction tells us something cannot be both A and non-A at the same time and in the same way. In other words, if I claim that it is now raining hamburgers from the sky, and you claim it is not, only one of us can be right (and I bet you know which one).

Religions Differ Greatly in Their View of God or Reality

Now that we have a little logic under our belt, let's consider some actual religious claims. What do world religions claim about God or ultimate reality? Here we discover several contradictory claims that, as we learned above, cannot both be true.

The Bible describes God as one, all-powerful, all-knowing Creator and sustainer of the universe.[1] We discover that He possesses perfect justice and yet is compassionate.[2] We learn from the pages of the Bible that God is a personal being and that He loves the world. In fact, we learn that love resides in the very nature of God.[3] We also find that it is possible to know God and that He rewards those who eagerly seek relationship with Him.[4]

Jews, Christians, and Muslims agree that there is only one God, and their religions are therefore called monotheistic religions. But other religions differ greatly on this belief. For example, the Zoroastrians believe there are two competing gods, one good and one evil. Ancient tribal religions, Santeria, Shinto, and some Hindus believe there are many gods (perhaps even millions of gods in some forms of Hinduism). The Taoist believes that there are two opposing impersonal forces represented in the drawing of the yin yang. Some Buddhists

---

1   Deuteronomy 6:4; 1 Chronicles 29:11-12.
2   Isaiah 30:18.
3   John 3:16; 1 John 4:7-8.
4   Hebrews 11:6.

believe there is a godlike impersonal force of which everything is a part, while others (like the Zen Buddhists) don't believe in the existence of God at all. Here we find one of the areas in which many religions disagree: Is God one, two, many, or none?

In addition to disagreeing on the number of gods, religions differ greatly on the nature of God. Some religions view God as good; some believe in good and evil gods; still others believe God to be entirely indifferent to the world. While the Christian believes that God is love and personally interacts with people, the Buddhist would claim that ultimate reality is an impersonal force that has no qualities and cannot be described.

...religions actually offer contradictory ideas about the essential nature and identity of God.

Even those religions that agree that God is one disagree as to His characteristics and essential nature. The Muslim believes that God consists of a simple unity, while Christians believe God is one in essence yet three in persons.[1] The biblical notion that God eternally exists as Father, Son, and Holy Spirit is offensive to the Muslim and considered to be "shirk" or the greatest of sins. The Muslim god cannot "empty himself" and become a humble human in order to demonstrate his love.[2] They believe this would reduce his absolute transcendence and authority. What is more, though some references within Islam refer to god "loving" people who love him, we also read in the Koran, "Allah loves not those who do wrong."[3] By contrast, the Bible tells us: *In this is love, not that we loved God, but that He loved us and sent His Son to be the propitiation for our sins.*[4]

So here again we find contradictory claims: Is God essentially

---

1   Matthew 28:19.
2   Philippians 2:5-11.
3   Koran, Surah 3:140.
4   1 John 4:10 (NASB).

good, evil, or indifferent? Does God love all or only some? Is God knowable or impossible to know?

Religions Differ in Their View of Humanity

In the Bible, we read that God created humans in His own image and created them for relationship with Him. Both men and women were created in God's image, and both were capable of a relationship with God from the very beginning.[1] Thus, all human beings have ultimate worth, whatever their gender, race, religion, economic status, or favorite sports team. All human beings bear the image of God; all are loved by Him. Yet we also discover in the Bible that all humans fall into sin; all have become separated from God. *But your iniquities have separated you from your God*, says Isaiah.[2] Through one man, Adam, sin has passed to all human beings.[3] Sin has broken the relationship with God and caused a great divide between God and us. Sin has stained us in such a way that no amount of good work can erase the impurity we have imbibed. If a friend offered you a glass of water and told you it contained "only a few drops" of poison, would you drink it? Our sin is like this poisoned water, affecting our whole life. Because of God's perfect justice, something needs to be done to pay this penalty and clean this impurity. So, as the Bible describes humans as deeply flawed by sin, it also shows us that God loves us and sees our worth.

By contrast, the Buddhist believes that humans consist of an impermanent collection of illusions. There is no concept of the image of God or of the worth of the individual. The problem that humanity faces is one of attachment to the illusions of individuality.

The Hindu also believes that humans' primary problem is one of ignorance. For the Hindu, this ignorance extends to our

---

1   Genesis 1:26-27.
2   Isaiah 59:2.
3   Romans 5:12.

nature and our perceived individual self. Hindus claim that we must realize that we are merely extensions of the ultimate and impersonal principle. We have no individual importance or worth, but exist to be subsumed back into the ultimate principle.

For the other monotheistic religions, the ideas about humanity are also quite different from those of the Bible. For example, while the Jewish religion teaches that humans are made in the image of God, nationality and heritage as a Jew is important to understanding their identity and the chance of being chosen for salvation. There is no idea of sin dwelling in a person for the Jew, but instead our problem merely consists in failure to obey the Law of God.

The Muslim similarly believes that humans are created by Allah and capable of choosing to obey or disobey. The problem of humanity is failure to listen, submit, and obey the commands of Allah.

So which notion of humanity is correct? Are we merely collections of matter, extensions of an ultimate principle, or individuals made in God's image? Are we loved by God or is the universe indifferent to our existence? Is our primary problem one of ignorance, failure to obey, or sin? These views stand in opposition to one another; they cannot all be true.

 Religions Differ in Their Idea of Salvation

The Bible describes the pathway for restored relationship with God. *For Christ also suffered once for sins, the righteous for the unrighteous, to bring you to God.*[1] God Himself paid the penalty for our sins because we were incapable of paying for it ourselves. *He saved us, not because of righteous things we had done, but because of his mercy,*[2] writes Paul to Titus. He bridged the gap that we had created from our sins and made a way to

1   1 Peter 3:18.
2   Titus 3:5.

rescue us. *For it is by grace you have been saved, through faith – and this is not from yourselves, it is the gift of God.*[1] We cannot work hard enough to gain favor with God or to erase our sins, yet through faith in Jesus, our relationship with God can be restored, and our righteousness made new.

Consider how this idea of God's grace on our behalf stands in opposition to many of the world's religions. The Jewish religion teaches of the justice and mercy of God, yet provides no solution for a lawbreaker. Those who keep the Law of God perfectly can hope for heaven, yet those who break the Law (those who sin) have no clear path for salvation except to hope for God's mercy. Even the Jewish King David realized this when he committed adultery and murder. He admitted that the sacrificial system was not enough, but hoped that God could provide a way to offer him mercy.[2] The apostle Paul writes that only in Jesus can David's hope for forgiveness be realized.[3]

We cannot work hard enough to gain favor with God or to erase our sins...

Similarly, the Muslim must work very hard to obey and submit to Allah. The only way to achieve salvation for the Muslim is through personal effort and following the Five Pillars. These pillars include recitation of the *shahada* ("There is no god but Allah, and Mohammad is his prophet"), prayer five times each day, fasting (especially during the month of Ramadan), the giving of alms, and making a pilgrimage to Mecca. Even following these pillars does not guarantee salvation. In the end, one's good deeds must outweigh one's bad deeds to be considered worthy of salvation. The Muslim knows nothing of the idea of grace, hoping instead that Allah will overlook their minor faults and deem them worthy of heaven. As one Muslim friend recently

---

1   Ephesians 2:8.
2   Psalm 51:16.
3   Romans 4:6-7.

told me, "Allah can have mercy on little sins, but for big sins, there is no mercy at all."

Likewise, for the Hindu, salvation depends upon personal effort. An individual's works will follow them forever, even into the next reincarnated life. The quality of the next life will depend upon how many good and bad deeds were done in this life. The seemingly endless cycle of rebirth and reincarnation will continue until the Hindu can escape the world of experience through extreme religious devotion and separation from the world.

The Buddhist believes something similar in that karma follows each person into the next phase of reincarnation.[1] The Buddhist's hope rests on their ability to remove all desires and attachments from this life and realize their own nonexistence. The Buddhist must work diligently throughout each reincarnated life to achieve this state by effort of the will, denial of all desires of this world, and by the work of meditation. Dean Halverson writes, "The emphasis is placed on the *path* that *we* must walk. In other words, to the Buddhist, salvation is based on human effort. We are the ones who must strive to make it up the mountain."[2]

Here we find even more contradictory claims. Is salvation by works or is it by the grace of God? Can we work hard enough to attain our own way to heaven, or do we need God to initiate a rescue on our behalf?

Religions Differ in Their View of Eternal Destination
In the Bible, we discover that it is possible to know where we will go when we die. *And this is the testimony: God has given us eternal life, and this life is in his Son. Whoever has the Son*

---

1   A strange contradiction appears here. As discussed above, many Buddhists and Hindus do not believe that there is a real individual soul. So when Karma follows the soul of a person, what exactly does it "follow?"

2   Dean C. Halverson, ed., *The Compact Guide to World Religions* (Minneapolis, MN: Bethany House, 1996), 62.

has life; whoever does not have the Son of God does not have life. *I write these things to you who believe in the name of the Son* *of God so that you may know you have eternal life.*[1] The Bible doesn't give many details about heaven, but we can learn that we will be with God; there will be no more death or mourning; God will wipe all our tears away; we will be able to interact and relate; there will be rewards; and there will be people from every nation and language there.[2] The Bible calls this hope of heaven *an anchor for the soul.*[3] Because salvation depends on the work of God rather than on our good works, we can be assured of heaven through faith.

Consider by contrast what the Muslim believes. The Koran describes paradise as a destination where physical pleasures will be plentiful. If one arrives there, they will enjoy "an ideal desert oasis with fruit trees, shade, refreshing drinks, and beautiful companions."[4] Yet one can never be sure they will reach heaven, since salvation depends upon the amount of good works one has accrued. The only way to be sure of entering paradise is to live a perfect life or by performing jihad. I asked some of my Muslim students in class once to describe what this would be like, and they answered that Allah would take out a scale and weigh all the good works and bad deeds to see which was heavier. Even then, they admitted, Allah could decide whatever he wanted and send them wherever he wanted. Thus, the students acknowledged that they could never be sure they would reach paradise.

The Hindu and Buddhist look forward to an even more distinct destination. Both of these eastern religions use the term *nirvana* to refer to the ultimate desired destination. The term

---

1   1 John 5:11-13.
2   Matthew 6:4; 16:27; Revelation 7:9; 21:4.
3   Hebrews 6:19.
4   Winfried Corduan, *Neighboring Faiths: A Christian Introduction to World Religions* (Downers Grove, IL: InterVarsity Press, 2012), 93.

nirvana means "blown out," and in both of these religions, reaching this goal includes the realization that one's own identity and existence are merely illusions.

For the Hindu, nirvana represents a state of bliss where one has escaped the cycle of rebirth and reincarnation and has risen above the world of experience to unite with the ultimate state or place of existence. Nirvana represents a state in which experiences and individual self no longer exist; instead, "like a drop of water joins the ocean," one's individual soul disappears into the ultimate state. Extreme devotion and separation from the physical world is the only way to arrive at this destination.

...the road to New York does not lead to London, nor Tehran, nor Tokyo.

The Buddhist goes even further, describing this state as non-existence or even extinction of the self. The Buddhist's ultimate reality is truly *nothing*. There is no god or being to unite with, nor is there a supreme principle per se. Instead, ultimate reality is a void of nothingness. Those who reach this nirvana have no experiences, no individual thoughts, no bliss or pleasures. One arrives at this destination through meditation and removing all attachments, all desires, and all ideas of individuality. Just like the Muslim, the Hindu and the Buddhist must work very hard to attain salvation. Only through personal struggle, countless rebirths and reincarnations, and strict devotion could anyone hope to achieve salvation.

Again, here we discover that the world's major religions are heading in very different directions. They are not all trying to reach the same rooftop by way of different methods. Instead of describing different pathways to the same destination (like Sri Ramakrishna's stone stairs, rope, or bamboo pole), these world religions aim at entirely different destinations. Some have said, "All roads lead to Rome," or "All paths lead to God." But we need to remember that the road to New York does not lead to London, nor Tehran, nor Tokyo.

Jesus' Exclusive Claims

Jesus made some very exclusive claims, but all religions make exclusive claims. For example, the Buddhist belief that God does not exist rules out the belief that God exists. The Muslim belief that God cannot be identified with any human creature rules out the belief in the incarnation of Christ. The Jewish idea of keeping the Law rules out the idea of salvation by grace. The Hindu idea of the plurality of gods rules out the notion that only one personal God exists. Even the narrator of the blind men and elephant story we examined at the beginning of the chapter makes an exclusive claim to know how all the claims of the blind men fit together. The idea that Christianity is exclusive while other religions are inclusive is simply wrong.

To make the claim that all religions teach the same thing, one must actually take a disrespectful position toward other religions. In other words, to be a religious pluralist, one has to believe that each religion *does not really mean what it claims.* So, when the Christian claims that God exists and the Buddhist claims that God does not exist, the pluralist must change one or the other contradictory statements in order to harmonize these ideas. He may claim that the Christian uses the word *God* to describe an impersonal principle or idea, but this is not what the Christian means at all. Or, conversely, the pluralist may attempt to show how the Buddhist idea of nonattachment is simply a form of being a good person and obeying God. But this is not what the Buddhist means at all. How would you feel if you claimed to be hungry for pizza, yet your friend "interpreted" your desire and claimed, "You are not really hungry for pizza, but instead you are trying to express your need for exercise."

This kind of reinterpreting does not help us to understand one another but merely shows disrespect and misunderstanding.

So what did Jesus actually claim? After feeding the five thousand, He declared that He was the Bread of Life and those who came to Him would be satisfied. When questioned about healing a man born blind, He claimed to be the one capable of making all people see. He claimed to be the Good Shepherd and demonstrated this by laying down His own life for the sheep. He claimed to be the resurrection and the life, holding the power of life and death in His own hands. He backed this claim up by raising Lazarus from the dead. He also claimed to be the way, the truth, and the life, and the only way to reestablish relationship with the Father. Why would Jesus make such an exclusive claim? This question can only be answered by considering our true problem as human beings. If our problem is ignorance, perhaps we merely need education. If our problem is failure to keep the Law, we need to try a bit harder. But if, as the Bible claims, we are dead in sin and are suffering from a broken relationship with God, the only solution can be real reconciliation.

Imagine the drama playing out behind the scenes in Genesis as Satan contemplates how to defeat a God who is perfect in love and perfect in justice. "Perhaps," he schemes, "if I can entice the object of His love to violate His justice, God will be locked in an eternal dilemma." Indeed, in Genesis 3, the creatures God created and endlessly loved violated His commands and poisoned themselves with sin. How could He solve such a dilemma? His eternal justice demanded a payment, yet His eternal love desired a merciful solution. In the ultimate answer to this dilemma, God sent Jesus. *But God demonstrates his own love for us in this: While we were still sinners, Christ died for us.*[1] Jesus' death satisfies God's justice as the perfect sacrifice for

---

1   Romans 5:8.

the human race. At the same time, God deeply demonstrates His great and eternal love. Jesus then invites us back into His family, back into relationship with God through faith. In Christ, God accomplishes justice, demonstrates love, and restores the broken relationship. Could there be any more profound demonstration of the perfect plan of God?

How are we to accept this invitation? The Bible teaches that asking God for forgiveness and putting one's faith in Jesus will allow us to enter into relationship with Him. *Yet to all who did receive him, to those who believed in his name, he gave the right to become children of God.*[1] The Bible instructs us that faith is the only requirement for salvation. Rather than excluding many, this actually makes the way open for anyone to come to salvation. If God were to require a certain amount of good deeds, only those who had the opportunity or life span to accomplish such deeds could be saved. If God were to require knowledge of a certain number of propositions, only those with capacity and opportunity to understand these higher truths could be saved. If God were to require nationality, language, pilgrimage, or effort, many people would be excluded. Instead, God simply requires faith, and opens the door of salvation to all people, regardless of mental capacity, opportunity, life span, ethnic or social background, or even religious upbringing.

Can God Save Anyone?

What about those from other religions or faraway countries who never have the chance to hear about Jesus? Since Jesus claims to be the only way to God, is God limited in His ability to offer salvation to them?

First, the Bible explains that all people have access to basic knowledge about God as revealed in nature. Just looking around outside is enough, says the apostle Paul, to remind us

---

1   John 1:12.

that God exists and is powerful.[1] This knowledge is enough to allow people to recognize their need for God.

Second, the Bible gives examples of God reaching out to people from other religions with the gospel. For example, Cornelius is described in Acts 10 as a God-fearing Jew. Instead of leaving him where he was, God goes to great lengths to communicate through angels to Cornelius that he must find Peter to hear the good news. Examples of God's work in this way abound in the Muslim world today as people see visions, have dreams, and are drawn to Jesus Christ. An international student once asked me about his family members. Since they lived in a distant and "closed" country, how could they hear the gospel and be saved? I asked a mentor how to respond to this question, and his answer surprised me: "Well, I would say that God figured out how to save you. Don't you think He can figure out how to save your family?"

Finally, because of the payment of Christ, God is justified in saving anyone He wants; no one is outside of the possibility of God's salvation.[2] Paul takes up this question in Romans 4 when he asks about Abraham, who lived too early to know the name of Jesus. Abraham was still saved through faith; Abraham believed everything that God revealed to him. Paul argues that the blood of Christ enables God to save Abraham and anyone else. This does not mean that all will be saved, but merely that no one is too far away, too isolated, too separated by distance, time, knowledge, or anything else to be saved. *Surely the arm of the* LORD *is not too short to save,*[3] writes Isaiah. No one is outside God's power to save.

That being said, God has given *us* the great privilege of sharing our faith with others. His primary method of bringing people to salvation seems to be through the preaching of the gospel

---

1   Romans 1:20.
2   Romans 3:25-26.
3   Isaiah 59:1.

and people's response of faith. Thus, we have a great privilege and a great responsibility. Paul exhorts us to get involved in this opportunity by saying, *How, then, can they call on the one they have not believed in? And how can they believe in the one of whom they have not heard? And how can they hear without someone preaching to them?*[1] What could be a higher calling than to join with God in His reaching people with the gospel? *"How beautiful are the feet of those who bring good news!"*[2]

> No other religion invites us back into relationship with God through faith.

Furthermore, God actually desires that people come to repentance. The Bible claims, *You will seek me and find me when you seek me with all your heart.*[3] This is a wonderful and amazing claim. If we are to believe it, we must conclude that no one who honestly, passionately, and wholeheartedly pursues God will fail in their pursuit to find Him!

Conclusion

The Bible presents a clear picture of the nature of God, our created value, and our primary problem. It also presents the solution to our problem and provides assurance of salvation and eternal hope. Other religions offer very different and contradictory claims about the nature of God or reality, about our primary problem, and about what we must do to solve this problem. Rather than all teaching essentially the same thing,

---

1   Romans 10:14.
2   Romans 10:15.
3   Jeremiah 29:13.

the religions of the world offer different hopes and aim at very different destinations.

Jesus offers, *Come to me, all you who are weary and burdened, and I will give you rest.*[1] No other religion in the world gives us the same invitation. No other religion answers the deepest questions regarding the great worth of every individual but still accounts for the depth of evil found in the human heart. No other religion offers such a sublime solution to this dilemma as God Himself come down to us as a sacrifice of atonement. No other religion invites us back into relationship with God through faith. To claim that all religions teach the same thing is to miss this incredible and unique truth. Indeed, *Salvation is found in no one else, for there is no other name under heaven given to mankind by which we may be saved.*[2]

Discussion Questions

- In your conversations with those from other religions, what similarities do you find between their beliefs and yours? What differences do you find?

- Do you think making an exclusive claim about the nature of reality is arrogant? Why or why not?

- How can one make an exclusive claim gently and respectfully?

- What are some good questions you could ask one of your friends from another religion to find out more about what they believe and engage them in further dialog and discussion?

---

1   Matthew 11:28.
2   Acts 4:12.

Chapter 8

Has Science Disproven God?

By Craig Reynolds

The heavens declare the glory of God; the skies proclaim the work of his hands. Day after day they pour forth speech; night after night they reveal knowledge. They have no speech, they use no words; no sound is heard from them.
(Psalm 19:1-3)

Charlie's leg bounced as he sat in the tiny desk in Shelby Hall waiting for class to start. In ten minutes, he would officially begin his college career – Biology 114 with Dr. Jason Toledo. He was more than a little nervous. Dr. Toledo had a reputation for being difficult, especially with Christian students in his class.

The first few minutes went well. Dr. Toledo worked through introductions and the course syllabus; then he jumped into his first lecture. "All living organisms exist due to natural causes," he began. "I'm sure many of you have been taught some all-powerful Santa Clause in the sky called God created everything, but you have been misinformed. No matter what your well-meaning Sunday school teacher or third-grade-educated grandparent has told you, God is not necessary to explain the natural world and how it works. It is my job to make sure you understand this important point."

Charlie could feel his face turning red and hoped Dr. Toledo didn't notice the sweat forming on his brow. He knew some people at this state university would disagree with his Christian worldview, but he was surprised to encounter such a hostile challenge so early into his college experience. How could his faith endure this class, which would teach how science makes his belief in God obsolete?

To begin this discussion, we must remember the Bible was not written as a scientific textbook to provide detailed explanations for how the natural world works. Rather, the Bible is God's revelation to mankind to reveal His character and work in the world, namely His free offer of salvation through the person and work of His Son, Jesus Christ. In contrast, the purpose of science is to use various tools and tests to provide an explanation of the physical world. But this does not mean that science and theology or philosophy have nothing in common. In fact, these disciplines of learning are at their best when they are in dialog.

...when science claims to say all that needs to be said, progress in learning is stunted.

As an example, scientists observe that all electrons have the same properties, such as charge and mass. Electrons differ from one another only numerically. But if two electrons, A and B, share all of the same properties, what makes them two distinct electrons instead of one? This is called the problem of individuation, and it is primarily a philosophical problem, not a scientific one. This means science cannot get far in solving this problem without relying on philosophy.[1] Sadly, when science claims to say all that needs to be said, progress in learning is stunted.

We must also understand that science is not the only source of knowledge about what is true – a view called scientism. This view is presented in two versions: Strong scientism holds that science is the *only* source of knowledge about reality, and weak scientism says science is the *best* source of knowledge. This view is self-refuting because science cannot prove this claim. If science is the only, or best, source of knowledge, then other areas of learning, including theology and philosophy, would only be matters of opinion or belief. With this mindset, it does not matter if theology provides truth of how things really are, because scientism says the best that theology can offer a person is therapeutic support or false hope. When you hear the message, "You cannot know there is a God because you cannot put Him in a test tube or test your faith empirically," you are being exposed to scientism.

In reality, other ways exist to discover truths apart from the tools and methods of science. Science can only study what exists in the physical world. This makes science a critical pursuit, and people are the beneficiaries of scientific advancements. We need to recognize that science cannot explain some things; neither can it verify or disprove certain truths.[2] As an example, I cannot scientifically verify that I love my kids, but I know that I do. I cannot scientifically prove that rape and murder are wrong, but I know they are. I cannot use the scientific method to demonstrate that something cannot come from nothing, but

---

1   J. P. Moreland, *Christianity and the Nature of Science: A Philosophical Investigation* (Grand Rapids, MI: Baker Books, 1989), 51.

2   For example, science will never be able to fully explain the origin of life and the universe. Science can only study the physical world *after* it exists, when it is available to examine. The question about the origin of the universe is a theological and philosophical question.

I know this is the case. There are other sources of knowledge and tests for truth than what is provided by science.

Each day, people just like Charlie face opposition for their faith in God and the Scriptures by people who believe that science and scientific discoveries nullify belief in God. A person does not have to be a college student to face these challenges, as contemporary media and pop culture tend to swoon over the latest scientific discoveries. This contemporary culture has come to believe that scientific evidence and explanations of physical matter will solve the world's problems. In this way, they replace any need for God. Scientific explanations can be intimidating to a Christian, especially when Christians feel unequipped to respond and wonder what the scientist knows that they do not. One might wonder if belief in God can withstand the rapid advancements and bold claims from much of the scientific community. Far too often people abandon their faith for lack of answers to science's persistent questions and doubts of theism.

Science and Faith Do Not Need to Be Enemies

Science and theism have more in common than is realized. They do not need to be considered opposing disciplines of learning, which is often the case today, as science is portrayed as ready to deliver the fatal knockout punch to theism.[1] We should understand that most of science is irrelevant to Christianity. For much of science and Christianity, there is nothing to argue about. For a Christian, it makes no difference if water is H_2O or H_3O. Christians and non-Christians use the principles of physics to design and build bridges the same way. The facts about our physical world are in place to be observed by both the theist and the atheist, and both accept the overwhelming

---

1   It should be noted that animosity has flowed in both directions, as church history has had seasons of opposition to science.

majority of these scientific facts in the same way. Science and Christianity are not archenemies.

A small portion of science, however, is problematic to Christianity and vice versa. These topics are significant, but they are often blown out of proportion, causing it to appear that all of science and Christianity are at odds. What are these areas of difficulty for science and the existence of God? The two points of conflict that receive a great deal of attention are the age of the universe and the explanation for how the universe began. Regarding the age of the universe, a steep discrepancy exists between a unified scientific community that holds the age of the universe to be about 14 billion years and Young Earth Creationists who say creation is only thousands of years old.[1] The second issue involves how the universe began. It centers on the debate between creationism and Darwinian macroevolution. Creationists hold the view that God created everything that exists. Evolutionists view the physical world, including life itself, as coming into existence without God.

In recent years, Darwin's theory of evolution as an explanation for the origin of the universe has been shown to be a deeply flawed theory.[2] This becomes evident as macroevolution gives an ad hoc explanation for how the universe began (that is, something came from nothing in a spontaneous, unintelligent, and unguided event), but cannot answer how this happened or for what purpose. For example, science can explain how the human eye works, and Darwin's evolutionary theory can provide a story for how the human eye came to be (that is, random mutations of prebiotic slime over enough time

---

1   It is worth noting that Day-Age Creationism, which is a biblical view for the age of the universe, does not have any conflict with scientific evidence that points to creation being billions of years old.

2   For example, see "Doubts Over Evolution Mount With Over 300 Scientists Expressing Skepticism With Central Tenet of Darwin's Theory," *The Discovery Institute: www. discovery.org/a/2114* and Henry M. Morris, "The Scientific Case Against Evolution," *Institute for Creation Research: www.icr.org/home/resources/resources_tracts_ scientific caseagainstevolution/.*

eventually formed into an eye), but science cannot explain why the human eye happened. Only with God can there ever be an explanation for why something exists. Atheist Bertrand Russell said, "Unless you assume a God, the question of life's purpose is meaningless."[1] In another example, Stephen Jay Gould famously stated:

> "We are here because one odd group of fishes had a peculiar fin anatomy that could transform into legs for terrestrial creatures; because the earth never froze entirely during the ice age; because a small and tenuous species, arising in Africa a quarter of a million years ago, has managed so far, to survive by hook and by crook. We may yearn for a 'higher' answer—but none exists."[2]

While some in the scientific community and Christian theology butt heads on a few topics, the majority of the time no conflict exists between these two pursuits. This means that a person should be able to comfortably hold to a Christian worldview and feel at home in appreciating or studying science. In fact, in many ways science is helpful to confirm faith in God's existence. The fine-tuning argument for the universe notes several ways the conditions of earth are precisely set for life to exist. Factors such as a twenty-four-hour rotation of the earth or its distance from the sun are all exactly what is required for life. Mathematician Donald Page reports that the odds of the universe randomly taking a form that is suitable for life are an astounding 1 in $10,000,000,000^{124}$! In other words, impossible.[3]

---

1   Bertrand Russell, quoted in Rick Warren, *The Purpose-Driven Life* (Grand Rapids, MI: Zondervan, 2002), 17.

2   James A. Haught, *2000 Years of Disbelief: Famous People with the Courage to Doubt* (Amherst, NY: Prometheus Books, 1996).

3   There are several other examples that could be provided such as irreducible complexity or the design argument.

How a Christian Can Pursue Science

Christians hold that all truth is God's truth. Because of this, they can comfortably pursue both science and a robust Christian faith. Historically, Christians have been on the cutting edge of scientific discoveries.[1] Sir Francis Bacon (the father of the scientific method),[2] Galileo, Blaise Pascal, Isaac Newton, and Michael Faraday were all committed Christians. The Christian worldview played a necessary and foundational role for their scientific thought and discoveries.[3] Some scholars have even postulated that it was due to the Christian worldview

...it was due to the Christian worldview that science rose to such prominence in the Western world.

that science rose to such prominence in the Western world. We have no doubt that history has demonstrated a rich and vibrant relationship between science and theism.

In addition, the Bible is not anti-science. It teaches that nature is real, unlike the teaching of Hinduism, which holds that all of reality is an illusion. Because nature is real, it can be studied. In addition, Jesus referenced science in His ministry. In His Sermon on the Mount, He referenced iridology, which is the science of determining health by examining the markings on an eye.[4] While this is an uncommon practice today, it was a primary medical practice in Jesus' day. Jesus told the crowd, *"The eye is the lamp of the body. If your eyes are healthy, your whole body will be full of light. But if your eyes are unhealthy, your whole body will be full of darkness.*[5] Here Jesus referenced a well-known medical practice to teach a spiritual lesson.

A Christian who appreciates or studies science must

---

1   Moreland, *Christianity and the Nature of Science: A Philosophical Investigation*, 17-21.
2   See *www.khanacademy.org/humanities/monarchy-enlightenment/baroque-art1/ beginners-guide-baroque1/a/ francis-bacon-and-the-scientific-revolution* (July 14, 2015).
3   Moreland, *Christianity and the Nature of Science: A Philosophical Investigation*, 44-45.
4   Bernard Jensen, *The Science and Practice of Iridology* (Warsaw, IN: Whitman Publications, 2005), i.
5   Matthew 6:22-23.

understand the criticism that will likely come their way and be able to respond. First, a believer must understand that science itself does not disprove the existence of God. Often when people claim that science has disproven God, what they mean is the scientific method cannot substantiate His existence, so He therefore must not exist. But the question of God's existence cannot be answered by the scientific method, because it is not a scientific question. In fact, when scientists claim their work has disproven God's existence, they are making a philosophical claim, which cannot be substantiated scientifically.

Next, a Christian must recognize that a person's worldview plays a significant role when discussing faith and science. Some people, prior to examining the evidence, view the universe as God's creative handiwork, and others view it as a cosmic accident that came about through random, unguided natural processes. How can two people see the same world in such different ways? The answer: They each observe the world with different foundational worldview assumptions. If a person holds to a naturalistic worldview, they are predisposed to view the universe through completely natural means. They believe everything came into existence and evolved into its present form without God.[1] But if a person has a theistic worldview, they are comfortable in acknowledging God's existence and work in bringing about creation.

Neuroscientist and popular atheist Sam Harris acknowledges that only 12 percent of Americans hold to naturalism. This statistic bothers Harris, since he believes science has proven God is neither necessary nor plays a role in explaining the existence of the universe. Harris notes, "If our worldview were put to a vote, notions of 'intelligent design' would defeat the science of biology by nearly three to one. This is troubling, as nature

---

1   William A. Dembski and Michael R. Licona, eds., *Evidence for God* (Grand Rapids, MI: Baker Books, 2010), 28-31.

offers no compelling evidence for an intelligent designer and countless examples of unintelligent design."[1]

Despite naturalism being the dominant worldview among the scientific community, theism persists as the dominate worldview for most people. One of the primary reasons for this is that most people intuitively know that naturalism is incapable of answering several of life's most pressing questions, which are philosophical in nature:

What is truth?

What is moral?

What is the purpose of life?

How did life begin?

Science practiced with a naturalist worldview cannot give hope that life is not in vain and cannot offer any basis for morality or beauty. When asked how life first began, it can only provide a story of how all that exists spontaneously came from nothing. When a believer recognizes the dominant worldview in the sciences today is naturalism, they will understand the philosophical landscape and be able to navigate its challenges much more effectively.

How Did Life Begin?

One reason a Christian can have great confidence that science has not disproven God's existence is that something *cannot* come from nothing.[2] In 1953, Stanley Miller performed a famous experiment at the University of Chicago where he attempted to prove life can come from reactions in the atmosphere without intervention from God. Was he successful? No. First, Miller created an atmosphere for his experiment that did not include

---

1   Sam Harris, *Letter to a Christian Nation* (New York: Vintage Books, 2006), x.

2   Paul Copan and William Lane Craig, *Creation Out of Nothing: A Biblical, Philosophical, and Scientific Exploration* (Grand Rapids, MI: Baker Academic, 2004), 250-252.

oxygen. He did this because oxygen would have destroyed the amino acids, the building blocks of life. While this is fine for a lab experiment, it is not representative of the actual atmosphere. Oxygen has always been a part of the atmosphere. Geologists who point out that all rocks display oxidization verify this. In addition, the ozone layer cannot exist without oxygen, and without this protective layer, nothing would block ultraviolet (UV) rays from the sun. This is noteworthy because UV rays decompose ammonia. If there is no oxygen, there would be no ammonia, which happened to be one of the main ingredients used by Miller in his experiment. So, not only did Dr. Miller artificially remove oxygen, but he also actively maintained certain and specific levels of ammonia.

...their assumptions that something came from nothing contradicts the law of biogenesis.

The second problem with Miller's experiment is that he used artificial actions that did not replicate the natural environment. He engineered a spark to provide the energy needed to combine the molecules that form amino acids. Without amino acids, the proteins which serve as the building blocks of life would not exist. Even though the spark provided the necessary energy, Miller knew that adding the spark would actually destroy the amino acids, unless they were protected somehow. To do this, he circulated gases to trap the amino acids and protect them from the spark.

In the end, Miller's experiment did not produce life as it could have happened in reality. He actually proved something does *not* come from nothing. Even using the physical building blocks for life, it took a significant amount of engineering and active intervention from this very "intelligent designer" to achieve the results he desired. Miller's experiment only "worked" because an intelligence worked behind the scenes to manipulate the physical material. He was so desperate to support his naturalistic worldview that he ended up undermining it. Dr. Mark Eastman explains:

> "The major products of the experiment (tar and carboxylic acids) are poisonous to living systems. Such chemicals poison and ultimately kill living systems by binding irreversibly to protein enzymes in them. This is how modern pesticides kill their prey. In fact, had he drunk the solution his experiment produced, it is a virtual certainty that Stanley Miller would have died. To argue that such a toxic environment is the cradle of life requires a great deal of faith."[1]

The results of the experiment cannot be used as evidence that life can begin from non-living matter. The results support the opposite conclusion.

Even other naturalists, such as Robert Shapiro, know this to be the case:

> "The very best Miller-Urey chemistry, as we have seen does not take us very far along the path to a living organism. A mixture of simple chemicals, even one enriched with a few amino acids, no more resembles a bacterium than a small pile of real and nonsense words, each written on an individual scrap of paper, resembles the complete works of Shakespeare."[2]

This experiment performed over fifty years ago is still highlighted in many high school and college textbooks to this day. Readers should not be led astray by Miller's experiment

---

1   Mark Eastman, M.D., *Creation by Design* (Costa Mesa, CA: Word for Today Publishers, 1996), 15.
2   Robert Shapiro, *Origins: A Skeptic's Guide to the Creation of Life on Earth* (New York: Summit Books, 1986), 116.

due to the faulty conditions he inserted into his work and his inaccurate conclusions.[1]

In addition, no matter how hard naturalists work, their assumptions that something came from nothing contradicts the law of biogenesis. This law states that living things come from other living things by reproduction. In effect, all life comes from other life. This proves that spontaneous generation, the idea that life can spontaneously arise from nonliving materials, is not only improbable, but it is also impossible. Nobel Prize-winning professor and philosophical naturalist George Wald (1906-1997) honestly admitted:

> The reasonable view was to believe in spontaneous generation; the only alternative, to believe in a single, primary act of supernatural creation. There is no third position. For this reason many scientists a century ago chose to regard the belief in spontaneous generation as a "philosophical necessity." It is a symptom of the philosophical poverty of our time that this necessity is no longer appreciated. Most modern biologists, having reviewed with satisfaction the downfall of the spontaneous generation hypothesis, yet unwilling to accept the alternative belief in special creation, are left with nothing. One has only to contemplate the magnitude of this task to concede that the spontaneous generation of a living organism is impossible. Yet here we are as a result, I believe, of spontaneous generation.[2]

Wald's position offers only two options for how life began. Either everything came from nonliving matter by spontaneous

---

1   For more detail on Miller's experiment, see *www.allaboutphilosophy.org/naturalism.htm*.

2   George Wald, "The Origin of Life," *Scientific American*, Vol. 191, No. 2 (New York: August, 1954): 46.

generation or some outside force performed an act of special creation. Even though Wald stated spontaneous generation was improbable, he still chose to support spontaneous generation as the explanation for the beginning of life. It would appear to require a great deal of blind faith to hold to a position when evidence demonstrates it is certainly false. Yet this is what is required for a naturalist who supports the idea that all matter came from nothing (a philosophical impossibility) and life came from nonlife (a contradiction of the law of biogenesis).

Is It Intellectually Lazy to Believe in God?

Earlier in this chapter, I quoted Sam Harris, a scientist and an atheist, who lamented the fact that roughly two out of three people believe that the universe exists because of the creative work of God with "no compelling evidence for an intelligent designer." Is he correct? Is there really no compelling evidence for an intelligent designer? Or are there scientifically consistent reasons to believe that an intelligent designer or God created the world?

Believing in the existence of God is not intellectually lazy nor scientifically dishonest. From science we can learn about specified complexity. This idea states that not only is the universe complex, but it is also specifically organized to maintain life. This reminds us that everything is working in order for a purpose. In the minds of naturalists, all the right parts would have had to randomly fall into all the right places at the exact right times for life to begin. As if the odds of this were not bad enough, these finely tuned materials must also maintain their form and function for an extended period to sustain life. For example, the moon is locked into a precise distance from the earth, so the two do not collide nor do the tides cause devastating flooding around the world.

Let's examine what makes the earth and the life that inhabits it a great piece of evidence for an intelligent designer, whom Christians call God. Considering intelligent design as an answer to scientific questions is not a loophole nor is it baseless. Many instances occur where intelligent design can be a logical suggestion. For example, in 1996 Michael Behe published *Darwin's Black Box*. In his book, Behe points out reasons to believe in an intelligence behind the irreducible complexity we see in the universe. Irreducible complexity is when a machine or substance consists of multiple parts, all of which contribute to the function. Without all the parts, the system ceases to function. One example that Behe used is the bacterium flagellum, the tail-like part of a bacterium. William Dembski and Jonathan Wells describe the bacterium flagellum this way:

> "The flagellum is an acid-powered rotary motor with a whip-like tail whose rotating motion drives a bacterium through its watery environment. This whip-like tail acts as a propeller. It spins at tens of thousands of rpm and can change direction in a quarter turn. The intricate machinery of the flagellum includes a rotor, a stator, O-rings, bushings, mounting disks, a drive shaft, a propeller, a hook joint for the propeller, and an acid-powered motor."[1]

This amazingly complex flagellum requires all its parts to operate; if even one part is missing, it will not work. Now, according to Darwinian macroevolution, this machine would have evolved one piece at a time over a long period of time. As a result, as the nine parts of the flagellum identified above evolved into existence, the bacterium would have to sit idly by waiting, because it would not be able to propel itself without the flagellum in full development. But the bacterium would

---

1   William A. Dembski and Jonathan Wells, *The Design of Life: Discovering Signs of Intelligence in Biological Systems* (Intercollegiate Studies Institute, 2008), 149.

not have survived this arrangement. It had to be created at one time with intelligence for all the pieces to be in place and to work properly.

By Darwin's own admission, the flagellum destroys his theory of evolution. Darwin said, "If it could be demonstrated that any complex organ existed, which could not possibly have been formed by numerous, successive, slight modifications, my theory would absolutely break down. But I can find out no such case."[1] Michael Behe did find such a case, because the bacterium flagellum cannot work unless all pieces are in place. Therefore, it could not have evolved one successive piece at a time and still function correctly. By looking at the complexity and order of the natural world, one can make a reasonable and strong case for a master engineer who designed and maintains both living and nonliving objects that make up the universe we inhabit.

Many more evidences point to God's existence, but the primary point of this chapter is to show that there is another side to the story. Christians do not need to be ashamed of their belief in God, regardless of what the naturalists say. The complexity and specific order of elements offer good evidence of an intelligent designer behind all that exists.

All mankind has the opportunity to observe the work of God in creation. How they interpret that creation will differ, however. None of us were present when the universe came into being, so the best we can do is look at the evidence and try to come to the most logical conclusion. Some will conclude natural causes alone created everything, but others see the hand of God in the origins and sustenance of the universe. For the Christian, studying science can enhance the appreciation for God's immensity and their own smallness. Psalm 8:3-4 reads, *When*

> *By Darwin's own admission, the flagellum destroys his theory of evolution.*

---

1   Charles Darwin, *The Origin of Species* (Bantam Classics, 2008), 189.

I consider your heavens, the work of your fingers, the moon and the stars, which you have set in place, what is mankind that you are mindful of them, human beings that you care for them? This is a reminder that science has not disproven God; rather, it is a great way to get to know Him and His work in detail.

Why Should a Christian Pursue Science?

Christians should care about science because it allows them to know God, not only from His Word, but also through His world. Once we realize there are solid extra-biblical reasons to believe God created everything, we can look at the Scriptures with fresh eyes and bold faith. We can look at the world around us or into the sky above us with certainty that a Creator marvelously designed each part with grand purpose, so we would see His greatness. We live in an ordered universe that functions according to laws that God has put into place. Once someone understands there is a God who created everything and controls it as well, they can have the confidence to believe that there is a purpose in life and hope for the next life. Science has not disproven God, and because the Bible gives us a true account of the intelligent designer, we have reasonable evidence to believe the other truths it teaches.

Christians should pursue science because there is more to discover about our world. Each year volumes of new research come out that explain more about how our world works in areas of biology, chemistry, and physics. But more work needs to be done. Thomas Edison observed, "We don't know the millionth part of one percent about anything. We don't know what water is. We don't know what light is. We don't know what gravitation is. We don't know what enables us to keep on our feet when we stand up. We don't know what electricity is. We don't know what heat is. We don't know anything about magnetism. We have a lot of hypotheses about these things, but that is all."[1] While this quote from Edison is nearly a hundred years old, and scientific progress has been made on the topics he identifies, we still have much more to learn. Christians should be leaders in the scientific community as they pursue scientific truth and seek to find all the ways and reasons in the natural world to praise God.

We can learn a great deal about our God by studying His creation. The Scriptures tell us this in Psalm 19:1-4:

> *The heavens declare the glory of God; the skies proclaim the work of his hands. Day after day they pour forth speech; night after night they display knowledge. They have no speech, they use no words; no sound is heard from them. Yet their voice goes out into all the earth, their words to the ends of the world. In the heavens God has pitched a tent for the sun.*

When we study the expanse and expansion of the universe, we can have a better understanding of God's ultimate power and authority.

Science matters because it corroborates the Bible, especially when it describes God as a God of order and not chaos. This truth means God has created a universe to function with law-like precision, which allows scientific discovery and progress. In contrast, a naturalistic worldview provides a picture of a universe in chaos without meaning. Whether a person studies the planets and stars high above or the human body, a person will likely marvel at the design and complexity of what they observe. But God's creative design goes beyond what can be seen through a telescope or microscope; God has also designed the non-physical parts of a person, such as personality, conscience,

---

1   Alexander Beddoe, *Biologic Ionization As Applied to Human Nutrition*, 6th edition (Warsaw, IN: Whitman Publications, 2002), 17.

free will,[1] mind, and emotions. A naturalist cannot accept these non-physical parts of a person and must either deny they exist or explain them away as physical events. Yet intuitively people know this is not true. God has creatively designed each part of a person for a grand purpose, which includes the ability to know right from wrong, appreciate beauty, test ideas, create music, express love, and show compassion.

Conclusion

God has created and sustains all that exists. The Christian gets to study the universe and in doing so appreciates the beauty and complexity of God's handiwork. Science is a tool that allows a person to learn about God's world and find all the reasons to praise God for who He is and the work He does. We need not choose whether to love science or love God. A person can be a Christian and engage in science, and science can be a marvelous tool to build the faith of the Christian.[2]

Discussion Questions

- Can you distinguish between science and philosophy?
- What is the underlying theme of naturalism?
- Think back to the story at the beginning of the chapter. If you were in Charlie's position, how would you respond to the professor?
- Reflect on Psalm 19:1-4 for a moment. What are some examples of how you can see God's work in nature?

---

1   **Free will:** The ability to choose freely from external constraints and prior causes. This view opposes determinism.

2   Additional thanks to Dennis Moles and Laura Whitson for their contributions to this chapter.

Chapter 9

Why Would a Good God Allow Suffering?

By Ryan P. Whitson

The weight of life crushed Sean, and he did not know how much more he could take. For years Sean, also known as Pastor Sean, had been the go-to person when life's struggles hit, but now he was the one who needed help. As he sheepishly sat down across the desk from a counselor, he opened up: "It's been a tough five years for my family and me."

With this understated introduction, Sean began to recount a listing of his recent past: A painful series of events resulted in his resignation as pastor of his church. Stress multiplied as bankruptcy threatened due to his being out of work. He and his wife faced a family-wide battle with a disease, extreme exhaustion, two miscarriages, and a stillbirth. Finally, a freak accident resulted in a finger amputation.

Sean moved forward on the couch, looked at the counselor, and shook his head. "I just don't get it. Why does God allow people to experience so much pain and suffering, especially when they're trying to live for Him? And why is it that those who are cruel and dishonest appear to get away with whatever they want? I guess what I need to understand is if God created the world and He is in charge, why is it so evil?"

Every single person experiences pain and suffering. It is a common human reality and not something we can avoid. Author Henri Nouwen said it well: "Our life is full of brokenness – broken relationships, broken promises, broken expectations."[1] Murphy's Law states this more directly: "If something can go wrong, it will."

...atheists rely heavily on the problem of evil to support their worldview...

As a result, the stories of hurting lives show up everywhere. Accounts of human misery are printed on the front pages of the morning paper and are usually the lead stories for the evening news. Suffering is a theme woven into countless movies and expressed in the lyrics of an overwhelming number of songs. Pain is on display everywhere a person turns, whether in their own life or the lives of others whom they know and love. This reality leads to pressing questions from people around the world:

If there is a God, why doesn't He stop the madness and fix the mess?

Is God powerful enough to do something about my circumstances?

Does God notice or care about my challenges?

People ponder these real-life, legitimate questions from childhood to death. Sadly, many of the conclusions people reach are neither helpful nor true.

After my wife, Laura, was in a severe car accident, a lady from her church visited while she was bedridden and undergoing intense therapy. In an effort to make sense of Laura's situation, she offered, "You know, God is disciplining you."

---

1   Henri Nouwen, *Sabbatical Journey: The Diary of his Final Year* (New York: Crossroad Publishing Co., 1998), 123.

The words the visitor intended for healing burned into Laura's heart and led her in that moment to hit spiritual rock bottom. She concluded that if God treated people who tried to honor Him like this, she didn't want any part of Him. Was the lady from the church correct? Was Laura's reaction to God as the one who breaks hearts, shatters dreams, and wounds the people He loves fair and true?

The bottom line is that people in pain want answers. They want to know why they are enduring hurt. They want to know if there is a God. Can He make sense of their misery? Will He do something about it? My hope is that this brief chapter will encourage your heart and strengthen your conviction that in the midst of real pain and suffering, there are thoughtful reasons to believe God exists and is both good and in control.

An Age-Old Problem

The dilemma of the existence of pain and suffering and the focus of Pastor Sean's questions raised earlier is called the problem of evil. *If, as the Bible teaches, God is in control and loving in character, then why do evil and suffering still exist in the world?* This question has served as the most compelling argument for atheism throughout human history and to this day has persuaded people to doubt God's existence. For others, the problem of evil motivates skepticism, either questioning God's sovereignty or His goodness, or both. Some believe that either God is good but has no power to fix the evil and resulting pain, or He has the ability but is unloving and chooses not to act. Therefore, skeptics conclude that God either wants to help but can't or He is able to help but does not want to do so.

Interestingly, atheists rely heavily on the problem of evil to support their worldview, yet ironically, this argument actually promotes God's existence. Here is why: If there is no God, all that remains to explain the reality of evil (and the suffering that results) is the physical world. But mere bits and pieces of matter such as atoms, molecules, dust, and rocks have nothing to say about morality, evil, or pain. As a result, nothing is available to explain what is called evil. Yet this is not a satisfying answer, because most people cringe at sights such as the slave trade or barbarous murder scenes from terrorist networks around the world. Most people know real evil exists and are able to identify it, but without God it is hard to explain the cause of this savagery. For this reason, people who experience deep suffering will usually look to God, either as the rescuer *from* their pain or as the one responsible *for* it.

Has anyone been able to solve the problem of evil? Many people have concluded that the most common solutions fall into one of three categories: God is not in control, or God is not good, or evil does not exist.

God is not in control

First, some say the problem of evil is evidence that though God may exist, He is not sovereign. In 1978, a Jewish rabbi by the name of Harold Kushner published a book titled *When Bad Things Happen to Good People.*[1] The title of the book alone helped make this publication a best seller. In the book, Kushner suggested that evil must exist and that God is loving, but He is not in control. Kushner's notion of God is that He wants to help because He is kind, but is unfortunately limited. The author even suggests we pray *for* God, who is Himself growing and learning as we are.[2] But the obvious question remains: If we are to pray *for* God, why should we pray *to* God?

Another contemporary theological movement that redefines God's knowledge and control of the universe is open theism. This view holds that there are certain things about the future

---

1   Harold S. Kushner, *When Bad Things Happen to Good People* (New York: Schocken Books, 1981).

2   Lee Strobel, *The Case for Faith* (Grand Rapids, MI: Zondervan, 2000), 38.

God does not know – namely, He does not know the decisions free human beings will make. Therefore, God fully knows the past and the present, but not all future events. As a result, since God does not know all future events, He cannot be fully in control. In this scenario, God is learning and adapting right along with humans.[1] Sadly, the idea that God is loving but small, and kind but incapable, seems to be gaining popularity.

God is not loving

Others will say God is powerful and in control, but He is not loving and doesn't care much about the pain and suffering of humanity. When a devastating earthquake struck Haiti in 2010, an estimated 300,000 people died, and an already desperate and impoverished nation was driven further into despair. Since the earthquake, Christianity has been expanding in Haiti where more than half the population actively practices Voodoo. Linda Markee, a leader of Haiti Foundation of Hope, said, "My experience is that as Haitians have come to know the love of Christ, there has been a huge number of people who have left the Voodoo and turned to Christ."[2] The Voodoo god (Bondye) is considered the supreme being, but is distant and uncaring. As the people of Haiti experienced their darkest hours, they responded to the love of God as they saw the work of Christian missionaries who delivered aid and the gospel message.

This idea that God is distant and unloving is not only inherent to the Voodoo religion, but it is also a characteristic of many other religious systems that teach that gods are moody, petty, and cruel. These less-than-gods can be manipulated through

---

1   An excellent resource to learn more about open theism is *Divine Foreknowledge: Four Views*, edited by James K. Beilby and Paul R. Eddy.

2   Stoyan Zaimov, "Haitians Turning to Christ, Abandoning Voodoo Practices 2 Years After Earthquake," *The Christian Post*; *www.christianpost.com/news/haitians-turning-to-christ-abandoning-voodoo-practices-2-years-after-earthquake-68124/* (January 27, 2012).

human works, and the object of these religious games becomes doing whatever is necessary to gain the deity's favor. The result is always a form of bondage, legalism, pride, and despair, not to mention the confusion for the person who barters with the god by making all the right sacrifices but still experiences the sting of suffering.

Existence of evil

Finally, some in the world will say that evil, pain, and suffering do not exist. For example, Buddhists teach that pain and suffering are an illusion. As the Buddhist moves along the eight-fold path toward enlightenment, he or she will begin to understand that pain and suffering are neither permanent nor real. Popular TV icon Oprah shares these themes with New Age comments such as, "You can choose what happens to you" and "You are responsible for your life – the power of God is within you, above you, and through you. You control your life."[1] Lofty claims such as these push the idea that any person can transcend evil and the pain that results.

Unfortunately, believing either that evil is an illusion or that suffering can be avoided because of human will does not change the way the world actually works. Evil is real; just ask any Jewish survivor of a German death camp or a witness to the terrorist acts on American soil the morning of September 11, 2001. To say that pain and suffering due to evil are not real does not fit human experience. While denying that evil exists can be a tempting move to somehow protect God's character, holding this position in light of the reality we all experience in this broken and cruel world is difficult.

---

1   Craig J. Hazen, *Five Sacred Crossings* (Los Angeles, CA: Contend Publishing Group, 2012), 105.

The Reality of Evil As a Reason to Believe

Acknowledging that evil exists and causes real suffering best explains reality and is a helpful tool for rationally believing that God exists.

Having said this, I want to be clear: No adequate words exist to capture the sobering depths of human suffering throughout the world, which reminds people repeatedly that the world is not as it should be. School shootings, natural disasters, crime, homelessness, disease, war, hurricanes, terrorism, and rampant injustice are frequent indicators that evil is alive and well in the world. At the same time, expressions of self-sacrifice, humility, beauty, and compassion confirm that all is not lost; good still exists.

Saying the world is not as it *should* be is making a claim that requires support: How do we know the world ought to be different? Where does this idea that some things are evil and other things are good come from?

When a person feels appropriate moral outrage, they are presupposing a difference between good and evil. Yet today many people embrace the idea that there is no ultimate standard of right and wrong. This is called moral relativism. This position legitimizes freedom from moral responsibilities (though not legal responsibilities) with the simple refrain, "Who are you to tell me what is right?"

Where does this idea that some things are evil and other things are good come from?

One significant problem with moral relativism is that people do not live life this way. While some may enjoy moral relativism when it comes to their own lives and actions, they are often quite comfortable pointing out immorality in the lives of others. For example, if you ask a moral relativist if sexually abusing children or calculated murder is evil and wrong, they will likely say yes, especially if the victim is their loved one or themselves. But this moral assertion, that child abuse is wrong, stands in contradiction to their belief that there is no ultimate standard for right and wrong. If they hold consistently to their belief that no ultimate moral standard exists, they cannot say child abuse is actually wrong. They can only perceive it as wrong (or their collective culture arbitrarily holds this position). But this is not how most people think or live. It appears impossible, even for a moral relativist, to escape thinking as if moral truth, including the existence of evil, does exist.

So if we hold that evil exists (and, as a result, the world is not as it should be) and that what we call "good" is to be preferred to what we call "evil," the question remains: Where does this idea come from? To answer this we need to turn to the first book in the Bible, Genesis.

The Bible opens with an account of God's work of creating the universe. All that He created was described as good. This is important; the world God created was good and not evil. Another important fact from the Bible is that God created people with genuine free will. This means humans have the potential to choose life or death, to love God or walk away from Him, to practice evil or to do good. Therefore, while God did not create evil, He did create a world that allowed for the possibility of evil and the suffering that results.

Some might protest that this distinction in Genesis does not matter, since evil is still the end result. But the Bible's creation account is very important. While some may view God's decision to create a world with the potential for evil as a foolish risk, it was a necessary step for intimacy and true relationship between creation (humans) and Creator (God). By giving humanity the genuine ability to make real choices, people were given the ability to choose to love both God and one another. Without the ability to choose to love, we have no possibility of an authentic relationship, and it could be said that life is all about relationships.

Sadly, the simple possibility of the presence of evil in the world became a reality as Adam and Eve, the first couple, made the decision to disobey God and launch all of creation into a fallen condition of sin, suffering, and decay. At that precise moment, evil entered creation and the world ceased to be as it should be. After this deed, humans first exercised their newly cursed knowledge of good and evil: *"For God knows that when you eat from it* [forbidden fruit] *your eyes will be opened, and you will be like God, knowing good and evil."*[1] This is why most people can distinguish between what is excellent, lovely, beautiful, and true, as well as what is inferior, evil, wicked, and wrong.

The free choice of people brought evil into the world, and the free choices of people today to sin (disobey God's commands) continues the pattern of pain and suffering. In this way, the world is the way people have made it. But even in the despair of evil that riddles every life on this planet, there is hope. If evil exists, which it surely does, then good must also exist. If evil and good both exist, as they surely do, then these must be knowable and distinguishable such that an absolute moral law or standard must exist. And if an absolute moral law exists, then there must be an ultimate moral lawgiver, which must be God. In this way, even our experience and knowledge of evil and suffering can point a person toward God.

The world is not as it should be. Evil, pain, and suffering are real, and these conclusions are support for the existence of God. But this alone is not enough to satisfy most hurting people. They want to know something about this God; they want to know: *What is He like and can I trust Him?*

---

1   Genesis 3:5.

The Sovereignty of God As a Reason to Believe

The Bible teaches that God is sovereign, which means He is completely in control. God demonstrates His sovereignty in two important ways: He is able to keep people from harm, and He is able to redeem suffering. Both of these truths are important because any hurting person is not only looking for comfort, but they are also seeking a sense of purpose in the pain and rescue from it. A person needs to know that God exists and is big enough to handle any situation; without this, we have little reason for hope in the midst of pain.

Unfortunately, not everyone is willing to allow God to redeem their suffering.

God's sovereignty also means He has the best perspective on the painful experiences people endure. He sees and understands more than anyone, and He is not just a passive spectator with courtside seats to the events of a person's life. God sees because God cares and wants to help. God is not absent, distracted, or unloving, but wants to work for good in the midst of suffering. This has proved true in my own life. God has redeemed many painful experiences to help me know Him and mature. The book of Isaiah speaks to this when God says, *"For my thoughts are not your thoughts, neither are your ways my ways," declares the* LORD. *"As the heavens are higher than the earth, so are my ways higher than your ways and my thoughts than your thoughts.*[1]

God's sovereignty also means He is wise enough to know that we need some pain and suffering in our lives in order to bring some eventual good, though we may not understand. As an example, even Jesus learned obedience through His suffering.[2] Similar to a physical therapist working on an injured muscle or a dentist drilling on a bad tooth, some pain can be used by

---

1   Isaiah 55:8-9.
2   Hebrews 5:8.

God for great benefit in our lives. Only a sovereign God can take evil and, for those who love Him, bring good out of it.[1]

Therefore, God may actually allow some suffering to get a person's attention in order to make it work for good. Too often people build false personal belief systems, destructive habits, and busy schedules to intentionally avoid God and cope with life's hurts on their own terms. This kind of lifestyle is harmful in many ways. Yet God may lovingly use a person's pain to wake them from their sin slumber and show them their need for Him. In this way, God allows pain to alert a person to their need for God and turn them toward repentance.

To this point C. S. Lewis famously wrote, "God whispers to us in our pleasures, speaks in our conscience, but shouts in our pains. It is his megaphone to rouse a deaf world."[2] In the Old Testament, God often used tests and trials to get the attention of His people, Israel. For example, Deuteronomy charges Israel to *Remember how the LORD your God led you all the way in the wilderness these forty years, to humble and test you in order to know what was in your heart, whether or not you would keep his commands. He humbled you, causing you to hunger and then feeding you with manna, which neither you nor your ancestors had known, to teach you that man does not live on bread alone but on every word that comes from the mouth of the LORD.*[3] The testing in the desert, though a difficult time for Israel, was useful to rouse the attention of the people and awaken them to their dependence on God.

If a person is willing to receive this, tremendous potential for good can come from suffering, and only a sovereign God can make this happen. Unfortunately, not everyone is willing to allow God to redeem their suffering. Despite the fact that hurt can yield positive results in character development, spiritual

1   Romans 8:28.

2   C. S. Lewis, *The Problem of Pain* (New York: Harper Collins, 1940), 91.

3   Deuteronomy 8:2-3.

maturity, and potential impact in the lives of others, too many people still live to avoid pain and, when it comes, do not allow God to redeem it. Ultimately, a person can either struggle in their own efforts to manage their suffering or surrender to God's good work in their trials. Both instances are painful, but suffering without any redeeming purpose is useless and depressing.

The Love of God As a Reason to Believe

Not only is God in control and able to redeem pain and suffering, but He is also willing to do so. Because He loves, God has chosen to take on evil by entering His own creation to clean up mankind's mess.

The most powerful and startling evidence of this is Jesus Christ, the Son of God, who took on human flesh to live among people and die as the atoning sacrifice for sin. Throughout His lifetime, Jesus lived in humble circumstances and was familiar with suffering.[1] Because of His love for all humanity, He chose to experience the hurts people endure and become the solution to the problem of evil and the pain that results. He did this through His death on a Roman cross and His resurrection three days later.

The Bible, which recounts the good news about Jesus Christ's death and resurrection, also gives an honest portrait of the suffering people experience. For example, the Psalms provide worship lyrics that are dark laments such as, *From my youth I have suffered and been close to death; I have borne your terrors and am in despair.*[2] These kinds of words acknowledge the hurts people face, even among the righteous, and the words aim to bring comfort.

In the Scriptures believers are commanded to follow the pattern of Jesus Christ; the Scriptures provide comfort and hope

---

1   Isaiah 53:3.
2   Psalm 88:15. Additional Psalms of Lament: 38, 51, 102, 130, 143.

to those who are suffering. Paul wrote, *Praise be to the God and Father of our Lord Jesus Christ, the Father of compassion and the God of all comfort, who comforts us in all our troubles, so that we can comfort those in any trouble with the comfort we ourselves receive from God.*[1] The role and privilege of the church is to work to alleviate the suffering of others. Doing so is an expression of the love of God. Too often a skeptic will bring up the problem of evil and then not lift a finger to help feed the hungry or clothe the naked. Followers of Jesus, who are called to mirror God's character, are commanded to engage, not avoid, the hurting.

Finally, God demonstrates love by giving His promises. In Psalm 23, the Lord promises to be the Good Shepherd who will provide and protect the hearts of those who are His. In Lamentations 3:22-24, God promises compassion, which He renews each morning. One of God's greatest promises to those who trust in Jesus Christ is that pain is temporary. Suffering has term limits. The trials experienced today will end – in the future or when this life is over. The Bible teaches that the day will come when God will wipe away every tear and correct every injustice.[2] It is reported that Mother Teresa, a woman familiar with suffering, once said that in the light of heaven, the worst suffering on earth, a life full of the most atrocious tortures, will be seen to be no more serious than one night in an inconvenient hotel.[3] Similarly, Paul wrote, *What is more, I consider everything a loss because of the surpassing worth of knowing Christ Jesus my Lord, for whose sake I have lost all things.*[4] In God's grace, all suffering is temporary, and this is a tremendous source of hope.

---

1   2 Corinthians 1:3-4.
2   Revelation 21:3-4.
3   Loss of Soul quotes on depression at *www.lossofsoul.com/DEPRESSION/depression-quotes-en.htm*.
4   Philippians 3:8.

Solving the Problem

Evil is real, God is in control, and He loves. If a person holds these convictions, have they made any real progress in resolving the problem of evil? The answer to this question is yes. The problem of evil is only solved by the death and resurrection of Jesus Christ – the final solution. It requires that all three points (evil is real, God is sovereign, and God is loving) are true.

The apostle Paul tell us, *But God demonstrates his own love for us in this: While we were still sinners, Christ died for us.*[1] In the midst of mankind's evil activities, God shows His love and power by choosing to get involved. How? He sent His only Son, Jesus Christ, to be a sacrifice for sin. He was the sacrifice that destroyed death, restored hope, and made a way of escape from the clutches of evil. The grace of God offered through the death of Christ redeems our lives and provides hope in the midst of suffering. Christ's work of atonement on the cross restores a shattered relationship with God. And the hurting find the help, strength, and encouragement to persevere with Jesus Christ, the One who is familiar with suffering, abandonment, slander, persecution, torture, and death.

...all three points (evil is real, God is sovereign, and God is loving) are true.

During the summer of 2012, a deranged gunman walked into a movie theater ten miles from my home and opened fire, killing twelve and injuring dozens more. This event devastated communities throughout the Denver metro area and across the nation. We do not doubt that an event like this can be characterized as true evil. Does the cross of Christ make a difference in a tragedy such as this? Yes, for in these moments, as in all moments, Jesus invites any person to Himself and offers hope, healing, comfort, and the peace that surpasses understanding, as well as ultimate deliverance from the clutches of evil. For a

---

1   Romans 5:8.

time, people grieve and ponder how any human being can willfully commit such an evil act. The best answer is provided in four short statements: Evil is real and active due to the free will of mankind. God lovingly chooses to get involved in pain and suffering. Through the cross of Jesus Christ, God has sovereignly destroyed the power of sin, death, and evil. The day is coming when suffering will finally be defeated at the return of Christ.

The End of the Story

The gospel of John gives an account from the life of Jesus: *As he went along, he saw a man blind from birth. His disciples asked him, "Rabbi, who sinned, this man or his parents, that he was born blind?"*[1] Seeing a blind man, certainly a condition that involved suffering, the disciples questioned Jesus. Similar to the book of Job, the worldview of the disciples held that sickness and suffering were the consequences of sin. Because this particular blind man was born with his condition, they assumed he was paying the penalty for his parents' sin. The Bible does teach that pain and suffering are a result of evil, but it does not teach that the suffering a person endures is necessarily a direct result of their individual sin. Sometimes a person suffers as a consequence of another's evil choices or an apparent random natural event.

Regardless, Jesus gave a surprising answer to the disciple's question: *"Neither this man nor his parents sinned," said Jesus, "but this happened so that the works of God might be displayed in him."*[2] The man was born blind to accomplish God's work in his life. It was not a punishment for sin or a matter of chance. In a broken world, blindness was this man's opportunity to manifest God's good work and glory in and through his life.

The disciples saw the blind man as a prop for their theological

---

1   John 9:1-2.
2   John 9:3.

riddle, but Jesus Christ saw the blind man as a person whose handicap, a continual source of suffering, was a way to display the glory of God. As a result, Jesus spit on the ground, making a dirt paste, and placed it on the man's eyes. *"Go," he told him, "wash in the Pool of Siloam" (this word means "Sent"). So the man went and washed, and came home seeing.*[1] Interestingly, in the text, the blind man never asked to be healed, nor was he promised healing, but obediently he went to wash his face (even if his only reason was to get the mud off his eyes!). This act of obedience was not easy, as Jesus instructed him to blindly walk with mud on his face across a section of Jerusalem's busy streets to a specific pool of water to wash. Without assistance, this would be quite the feat, and he would be quite the spectacle to the passing crowds. But he obeyed and God was glorified.

We all prefer pleasure over suffering and comfort over pain. But we must understand that pleasure and comfort are not the primary goals in life. The focus of God's work in your life is not necessarily to provide health and wealth and make all your dreams come true. He does provide good things out of love, but not because He is obligated to do so. When people view God as a personal vending machine for unending happiness, suffering shatters inadequate and unbiblical ideas of who God is and creates confusion in the midst of the hurt.

University of Notre Dame sociologist Christian Smith points out that a rapidly growing religious worldview in America today is what he calls Moralistic Therapeutic Deism (MTD). Moralistic Therapeutic Deism teaches that the most important truth is that God wants people to feel happy, be nice, and avoid pain.[2] It also teaches that God declares He will not interfere with your life, but will be available to you when you need Him,

---

1   John 9:7.
2   Christian Smith and Melinda Lundquist Denton, *Soul Searching: The Religious and Spiritual Lives of American Teenagers* (New York: Oxford University Press, 2005), 162-171.

similar to an airman who keeps his parachute for emergencies, but naturally hopes he never has to use it. C. S. Lewis observed: "We want, in fact, not so much a Father in Heaven as a grandfather in heaven – a senile benevolence who, as they say, 'liked to see young people enjoying themselves,' and whose plan for the universe was simply that it might be truly said at the end of each day, 'a good time was had by all.'"[1]

I tend to agree with Lewis's observation. We tend to view pain and suffering as problems and not opportunities. People immediately look for fixes to the hurt and medication for the pain as opposed to lessons to learn. Yet with the proper attitude, a person can experience joy from God in the midst of suffering – a calm assurance that even though they don't like what they are going through, they know that in His power God will work all things together both for their greatest benefit and His ultimate purposes.

Job, the Old Testament character who was an undeserved victim of evil and pain to an unimaginable degree, is probably the most famous example of suffering.[2] The puzzling question throughout the book of Job is why this man who loved God was enduring so much hardship. At the end of the book, God shows up to answer Job's question. Surprisingly, the answer was *Himself*; God's response to Job's "why" question was His presence, and Job was satisfied. He encountered God, and that was enough. God allowed Job to suffer, not because He lacked love for Job, but to bring him to a place where he could experience the Lord in a more meaningful way. God wants our greatest good, and our greatest good is to know and love Him deeply. Pain and suffering are gifts in that they are one way for people to experience and know God intimately.

Yet at the end of the day, some will cry out in protest to it

---

1   Lewis, *The Problem of Pain*, 31.
2   Job was a man who loved God. He was a prosperous farmer living in the land of Uz, but who quickly lost his various livestock, ten children, and many servants.

all, "God, where are you?" And others will cry out in worship through it all, "God, there you are!" Know He is with you in the deepest moments of despair, loneliness, pain, and suffering. He is there; He is sufficient; He is strong; He is doing a good work; and He is not yet finished working in your life. So there are reasons to have hope. Romans 8:18 reminds us all: *I consider that our present sufferings are not worth comparing with the glory that will be revealed in us.*[1]

Conclusion

For those who hurt and suffer, hold tightly to God and endure the pain honestly. Run toward the Lord and not away, all the while feeling and expressing the full measure of anger, fear, and tears, understanding that the grieving process is a gift from God to heal. But you do not need to grieve like the world, which has no reasons for hope. Rather, grieve with a deep trust in God that He will work for your greatest good and His greatest glory and that you have the opportunity to emerge from suffering a better person. In light of these truths, suffering provides a reason to believe in a good, powerful, and real God.

Discussion Questions

- Has there been a time in your life when you have asked the question that titles this chapter: Why would a good God allow suffering?

- God is loving and powerful enough to redeem the painful circumstances we all endure. What is

---

1   Romans 8:18.

your opinion about this statement? If this is true about God, what difference should this make in your daily life?

- Consider for a moment that God does not exist. What explanation is there for the existence of suffering? Is there any possibility for hope in the midst of pain?

- After reading this chapter, what questions or doubts still remain regarding God and His allowance of human suffering?

Chapter 10

Did Jesus Rise from the Dead?

By Dennis B. Moles

J ohn and Phil have been friends since high school. They were
a bit of an odd pair: John was the pastor's son and a band
geek, while Phil was the son of a bank president and a basket-
ball star. But these were the least of their differences. John was
a committed follower of Jesus, and Phil an amiable agnostic.

Despite these differences, John and Phil built a strong and
lasting friendship that extended beyond their years at Mount
Vernon High School and into adulthood. But they could never
quite see eye to eye on one issue – the resurrection of Jesus. Phil
was never an angry unbeliever; he admired many things about
John's faith. He found the teachings of Jesus compelling, but
could never wrap his mind around the fact that John's Christian
faith was based on something so obviously impossible.

Phil's mom and dad became Christians through their relationship with John's family, when both boys were juniors in
high school. When Phil's family attended church, he tagged
along without much protest or enthusiasm. He found the pastor's sermons inspiring, but he couldn't get his head around
the miracle claims of Christianity – especially the resurrection.
How could someone commit to such an *illogical* faith?

Many people who follow Christ have friends like Phil. They're not hostile toward Christianity, but they don't see how intelligent people can believe in something as "farfetched" as the resurrection. No matter how many Bible verses we throw at them, they remain unconvinced that Jesus rose from the dead. Why? Because everything in their experience tells them people don't come back from the dead.

What can Christians do to have effective conversations with their doubting friends? First, they can hold tightly to their own faith,[1] which includes the literal bodily resurrection of Jesus Christ, an essential Christian belief.[2] Seeking to explain away the resurrection or harmonize it with a naturalistic view of the world only compounds the problem. Christians do not need to deny the resurrection to be reasonable people. This chapter will show that the resurrection claims of Christianity are logically consistent and are the best and most reasonable explanation for the historical facts surrounding the death of Jesus and the establishment of the church.

Second, Christians should not attack the doubts of their skeptical friends. For example, the resurrection does not make sense to those who hold to a naturalistic worldview.[3] Conversations will make little headway until we begin to see things from the other person's perspective. When Christians admit that an unbeliever's skepticism makes sense given their worldview, we are not saying that we agree with them but that we *understand* them. Modeling this kind of understanding will be helpful when asking our friends to see the facts surrounding the resurrection of Jesus from a different perspective.

Third, a Christian must refuse to offer "because the Bible says so" appeals to the Scriptures. This kind of argumentation will not convince doubters that Jesus really did rise from the

1   Jude 3.
2   Romans 1:4; 6:5; 1 Corinthians 15:3-42; Colossians 1:18; Philippians 3:10-11.
3   For a fuller treatment of the topic of worldviews, see chapter 6 in this book.

dead. A Christian must commit to a relational and conversational form of apologetics that presents the facts in a gentle and compassionate manner. This approach is not for the lazy or the faint of heart. It will demand a high level of familiarity with the facts of the resurrection, a willingness to think hard about worldview issues, and it will take time.

The Resurrection Watershed

The resurrection of Jesus Christ is a central and necessary component of the Christian faith. All four gospel accounts present the resurrection event and assert that Jesus of Nazareth was crucified on a Roman cross, died, was buried, and rose from the dead on the third day. The resurrection of Jesus is also affirmed by the apostles Peter and Paul, the biblical author James, and the writer of the book of Hebrews. Most notably, Paul asserts that the bodily resurrection of Jesus was a necessary and foundational doctrine for the followers of Christ in the first century.[1]

But the topic that concerns us most in this chapter is not that Christians believe in the resurrection nor that the Bible affirms the resurrection claims of the first believers. Our main concern is to offer a reasonable answer to a more practical question. That is, how can Christians expect people to believe something that is, in Phil's words, so *illogical*?

While Christians claim that their faith is rational, folks like Phil genuinely struggle to see how that is possible, when by our own admission Christianity is based on a belief that clearly opposes natural law. The primary purpose of this chapter is to help people like John have meaningful conversations with their friends who struggle to believe in the resurrection. So how do we make progress when our starting positions seem to be so far apart?

---

1   Romans 1:4; 6:5; 1 Corinthians 15:3-42; Colossians 1:18; Philippians 3:10-11.

Before Beginning the Conversation

Before beginning a conversation with a friend who doubts or refuses to believe in Jesus' resurrection, we need to know a few things. The first is that the question of the resurrection is not a question of logic. As difficult as it may be for some on either side of the conversation to understand, both Phil and John can logically defend their beliefs. Christians are often accused of being illogical, because they believe in supernatural truth, but that is not the case. To believe in something that cannot be scientifically verified is not illogical given the Christians' foundational belief in an all-powerful God. It merely does not fit within a naturalistic worldview.

To believe in something that cannot be scientifically verified is not illogical...

One of my favorite literary moments comes from C. S. Lewis's classic, *The Lion, the Witch, and the Wardrobe,* when Susan Pevensie tells Professor Kirke that she does not believe Lucy's tale about going to a land called Narnia via an old wardrobe because "logically, it's impossible."

To this, Professor Kirke replies, "What *do* they teach in schools these days?" He is aghast at Susan's statement, because there is nothing logically wrong or inconsistent with Lucy's claim.

The question at hand for Susan is not the probability of Lucy's journey, but the reliability of Lucy as a witness. If Lucy is a known liar, then Susan has good reason to doubt her story. But if Lucy is generally and consistently truthful, then logically what follows is not a lie nor overt deception but something else.

Most of the time when people say that a statement, idea, or belief is illogical, what they mean is that the idea under consideration does not make sense to them or does not cohere to their beliefs about what is true, possible, or real. Professor Kirke's point to Susan is that, given Lucy's repeated pattern of truth-telling and Edmund's repeated pattern of deceit, it makes it more reasonable to believe her no matter how fanciful her story. Susan did not believe Lucy because her story exceeded Susan's experience of what was possible. Her worldview did not have room for Narnia. Most doubters and skeptics don't believe the Bible's account of the resurrection for the same reason Susan didn't believe Lucy – their worldview does not have room for the resurrection.

Christians believe that the resurrection is possible, not only because the Bible says it happened, but also because we believe in an all-powerful God who is capable of bringing people back from the dead. Given the existence of God, the question for Christians becomes much the same as it was for Susan: Is the witness – in this case, the Bible – reliable?[1]

Second, both parties, the skeptic and the Christian, have the same finite facts and information to deal with. It's not that either side has some super-secret trump card. The disconnect in most honest and friendly conversations about the resurrection of Jesus will not ultimately be rooted in the facts. Most of the time people bring the disconnect with them in the form of their worldview.

Christians do not need to fear the facts, but instead need to become familiar with them. Meaningful conversations are not just gracious and relational; they are also based on truth. Effectiveness demands that we know the various arguments, approaches, and perspectives on the resurrection. A great place to start is to familiarize ourselves with what Gary Habermas and Michael Licona call *minimal facts*. According to Habermas and Licona, there are five pertinent facts that are nearly universally accepted:[2]

1. Jesus died by crucifixion.

---

1   See chapter 3 for a fuller conversation on this topic.
2   Gary R. Habermas and Michael R. Licona, *The Case for the Resurrection of Jesus* (Grand Rapids, MI: Kregel, 2004), Kindle Electronic Edition: Location 325-698.

2. Jesus' disciples believed that He rose from the dead and appeared to them.

3. The apostle Paul was suddenly changed from a persecutor of Christianity to a proponent of it.

4. The skeptic James (Jesus' brother) was suddenly changed.

5. The tomb was empty.

Nearly all informed scholars, believers and doubters alike, agree that these five facts are historically verifiable. These accepted facts are essential for discovering what is the most reasonable hypothesis surrounding Jesus' death.

Third, commit to think and listen carefully. Just because two people are talking in one another's direction does not mean they are having a conversation. Don't assume you know what someone is going to say before they say it. Do not interrupt. Allow the person you are talking with to finish their thought before you speak, and don't be afraid to ask for the same courtesy. Take notes if you need to. Don't move the conversation forward until you are both ready. Ask good questions. Restate what you hear the other person saying. Be willing to think hard about your own beliefs. If you are going to ask the other person to doubt their presuppositions, be willing to honestly question some of yours too.

Finally, always remember that you are trying to win a person, not an argument. Too often conversations turn contentious, because one or both of the participants seek victory rather than understanding. The goal of these conversations is to remove obstacles from people who are considering the claims of Christ, not place more in their path. We all must be careful not to become one of the obstacles we are trying to remove.

Starting the Conversation

Begin by listening. Acknowledge that the other person's doubts make sense given their worldview, but lovingly challenge them to consider whether their current beliefs about the resurrection offer the best and most comprehensive answers given the historical information. As we move through the conversation, we must help them see that their worldview likely has insufficient categories to thoroughly and effectively deal with the historical facts.

Not all doubts are created equal, and not everyone struggles at the same points. Listening allows us to discover what aspect of the resurrection our doubting friends are struggling with, so we don't answer questions they are not asking. But this is only the first of many steps. It then becomes our job to challenge those doubts and foundational beliefs with love and respect.

Most people who doubt the resurrection do so because they do not have a category for it within their belief system. It stands in contradiction to their foundational beliefs about how the world works. For this reason, followers of Jesus need to begin conversations about the resurrection by letting their friends know that their unbelief is completely understandable. While this admission may seem to undermine your case, it actually strengthens it. One of the most effective things you can do when starting a conversation with our skeptical friends about the resurrection is to express understanding for their doubts. Again, this does not mean you are agreeing that the resurrection is irrational. It only means that the first presupposition we must challenge is the belief that the resurrection is impossible.

> ...the first presupposition we must challenge is the belief that the resurrection is impossible.

Issue an Invitation, Not a Hostile Challenge

Successful conversations demand a measure of openness and trust. This openness to another's perspective is not the same as compromising a conviction. Many times it is simply a byproduct of active listening and concern for the eternal well-being of another. People cannot be argued into the kingdom of God. If winning an argument was a successful evangelism tactic, the Christian faith would have gained more ground than it has over the last hundred years. This does not mean that argumentation does not have a place in our efforts to witness. Even though people cannot be argued into the kingdom, most can be reasoned with. The key is to utilize our knowledge and influence in helpful rather than coercive ways by inviting our friends to do three things.

First, invite them to doubt their doubts. Is there any possibility that they might be mistaken in some of their assumptions about how the world works?

Second, is it possible that there is a better, more logical or more desirable way to approach the facts at hand? If a worldview is like a lens through which we see the world, all we are doing is asking our friends to try on our glasses for a bit.

Third, challenge them to consider the resurrection of Jesus in light of the possibility that a God who created and sustains everything might exist.[1] If there is no possibility that God exists, then the claim that Jesus rose from the dead is ludicrous. But if there is even the slightest chance that God exists, then the possibility of resurrection becomes a viable conclusion when dealing with the historical facts of Jesus' life, death, and reported resurrection.

Consider the facts

Kris and I had known each other for a couple years but were

---

1   See chapter 2 for more on this topic.

more acquaintances than friends. But that changed during the last varsity swim meet of the 2014 season. Our conversation meandered from our sons on the swim team to the boys' schoolwork to, in a surprising twist, our faith and the resurrection of Jesus. His son was taking a history class at the public high school, and he was shocked that the class included a unit on Jesus. Knowing my work as a pastor and theologian, Kris asked, "Dennis, is there really enough historical evidence to include Jesus in a public school history course?"

The answer to this question is a resounding YES. The reality is that there is a great deal of information. Roman, Jewish, and Christian ancient literature attest to Jesus as a historical figure who lived and ministered in first-century Palestine.[1] Virtually no serious scholars deny these facts about Jesus. Many of the Bible's claims about Jesus are disputed, specifically the miracles associated with His life and ministry, but the fact that He lived and ministered is universally accepted. Based on this truth – that Jesus lived and ministered in first-century Palestine – let's look a bit closer at Licona and Habermas's minimal facts.

The first of Dr. Licona and Dr. Habermas's minimal historical facts is that Jesus died by crucifixion.[2] This point is imperative because it establishes that Jesus actually died. And if Jesus died, how do we account for the eyewitnesses who reported seeing Him alive after His crucifixion?[3] While some still assume that

1   Habermas and Licona, *The Case for the Resurrection of Jesus*, Kindle Electronic Edition: Location 409. See also N. T. Wright, *The Resurrection of the Son of God* (Minneapolis, MN: Fortress Press, 2003). See chapter 3 of this text for more information about the historical evidence for Jesus.

2   Habermas and Licona, *The Case for the Resurrection of Jesus*, Kindle Electronic Edition: Location 320-694. Habermas and Licona include these five points in what they call their 4+1 "minimal facts" approach to dealing with the resurrection of Jesus. This is significant because Licona and Habermas seek only to use the information that possesses the highest degree of certainty and acceptance in their arguments. They contend that the first four points are all but universally accepted with the fifth fact, the empty tomb, being a near-minimal factor since it is less, although still widely, accepted then the first four.

3   See the women at the tomb in Luke 24:1-12; the disciples in the upper room in John 20:19-23; Thomas a week later in John 20:24-29; the five hundred, many of whom lived until the writing of 1 Corinthians 15:6; and the apostle Paul (Saul) in Acts 9:1. Habermas and Licona, *The Case for the Resurrection of Jesus*, Kindle Electronic

Jesus could have survived the crucifixion and simply walked out of the tomb, His crucifixion is widely accepted.[1]

The second of the minimal facts surrounding Jesus' death is a curious yet powerful one. This fact asserts that the disciples all believed that Jesus rose from the dead and went to their graves asserting as much. Even though many skeptical scholars are clear to point out that the disciples' fervent belief does not prove the resurrection, they cannot deny that Jesus' closest friends and ministry colleagues never recanted or changed their story about the resurrection. If Jesus did not rise from the dead, these men knowingly and willingly endured torture, persecution, exile, and hardship to perpetuate something they knew to be a lie. This leads us to ask not only if this is reasonable, but also if it is possible for a group that exceeds five hundred individuals to keep such a ruse going even when facing death.

If the resurrection did not happen, a lucid naturalistic explanation should exist for each fact.

The third and fourth historical facts are the conversions of two key first-century church leaders: the apostle Paul (formerly Saul of Tarsus) and James, the half brother of Jesus. Both of these men had experiences that produced a sudden and dramatic change in their lives.[2] Paul went from breathing out murderous threats against the church to becoming one of its leading voices.[3] And James, the half brother of Jesus, transitioned from skeptic to true believer in Jesus after His death on the cross.[4]

Finally, Jesus' tomb was empty. While this point does not receive quite the acceptance of the first four (Licona and Habermas

---

Edition: Location 410. Habermas and Licona list no less than five non-Christian historical sources that affirm the early Christians' belief that Jesus died and rose from the dead.

1   This is commonly called the "swoon theory."
2   See Acts 9:1-19 for Paul's (Saul's) conversion experience.
3   Acts 8:1; 9:1, 19-20; 13:1-3; 14:1-7; 17:1-18:11.
4   Matthew 13:55-56 and Mark 6:3; Matthew 12:46-50; Mark 3:31-35; Luke 8:19-21; John 2:12; 7:3, 5, 10; Acts 1:13-14; 1 Corinthians 9:5; Galatians 1:19.

call it a near-minimal factor), it still deserves attention.[1] Many would position this argument differently, because the empty tomb is a widely accepted fact regarding Jesus' bodily death and burial. There is no evidence that any of Jesus' opponents or accusers produced information that demonstrated Jesus did not rise from the dead. If the tomb was not empty or if the disciples had gone to the wrong grave, all their opponents would have had to do was produce the body or send people to the right tomb – neither of which happened.

Despite what some recent skeptics have asserted about the likelihood that Jesus' body was never buried, there is no evidence for this whatsoever. What we know is that Jerusalem was a relatively small place, and if the body of Jesus, who had been publically executed, had still been in the tomb, it would have been impossible for Christianity to spread in the city.

Why do these facts matter since none of them *prove* the resurrection? They matter because each of these points needs to be explained. If Jesus did not rise from the dead as Christians claim, a reasonable explanation for the above facts that do not appeal to supernatural means should be apparent. Armed with this information about foundational beliefs and historical facts, the Christian and the skeptic can begin talking *with* rather than *past* one another, as they look for the best explanation of the facts.

Progressing through the Conversations

The next step is to evaluate whether any of the objections offered by your skeptical friend can account for the minimal historical facts. If the resurrection did not happen, a lucid naturalistic explanation should exist for each fact. If no explanation can

---

1   Habermas and Licona, *The Case for the Resurrection of Jesus*, Kindle Electronic Edition: Location 616. They claim that roughly 75 percent of scholars accept that the tomb of Jesus was empty.

account for all the facts, perhaps the fault is not with the facts but with the foundational beliefs held by the skeptic.

Looking for a way out

Let's look at several common objections and offer some information that will help us have constructive conversations with our doubting friends. If our doubting friends are correct, their explanation for these minimal facts should be more logical, compelling, and reasonable than our belief that Jesus rose from the dead. But are they? Let's take a look.

Objection #1

The gospel accounts of the resurrection are full of inaccuracies and inconsistencies and cannot be trusted.

This objection is about the Bible's reliability.[1] Is the Bible a reliable witness to the facts or not? When intelligent people challenge the Bible's reliability regarding the resurrection, they generally cite inconsistencies within the gospel accounts. They ask questions like:

> How many women went to the tomb: one, three, or more than three (John 20:1; Mark 16:1-8; Luke 24:10)?

> Did the women see one angel or two at the tomb (Mark 16:4-7; Luke 24:4)?

> Did John and Peter run to the tomb or just Peter (John 20:3-10; Luke 24:12)?

> Did the women say *nothing to anyone* or did they tell this disciple (Mark 16:8; Luke 24:9-10; John 20:2)?

---

1   For a fuller treatment of the trustworthiness of the Scriptures, see chapter 3 of this book.

Did Mary see/meet Jesus after she and the others
told the disciples about Jesus' resurrection
(John 20:11-18)?

It is clear that the Bible is claiming something supernatural happened – something beyond our experience and beyond
what we would call possible under normal circumstances. But
does the miraculous nature of the claim automatically render
the witness unreliable? Not necessarily.

Even though we believe that all the Gospels are inspired by
the Holy Spirit and are authoritative, each author writes with
his own voice, out of his unique experience, and from a certain
perspective. Just as four witnesses standing on four different
street corners have different perspectives of the same traffic
accident, these four men have different perspective, goals, and
purposes in writing their accounts. Lack of uniformity is not
contradiction. Inconsistencies due to varied perspectives are
not always conflicting.

Luke set out to write an accurate and orderly account of
Jesus' life, ministry, death, and resurrection. He was not an
eyewitness to these events, but based his gospel on investiga-
tive research and personal interviews with eyewitnesses. Mark
tells the story of Jesus from the perspective of Peter and writes
to a primarily Roman audience. Matthew, one of the twelve
apostles, writes his gospel as a first-person witness. His primary
audience is the Jews, and his purpose is to show that Jesus of
Nazareth was the promised Messiah. John's gospel is distinct
from the first three. It is more like a memoir than a history. All
inspired, all authoritative, but all unique and meant to fulfill
a specific purpose.

So how do we handle the inconsistency objection? It may
seem overly simplistic to some, but the fact that Matthew,

Mark, Luke, and John are not uniform in their accounts is not problematic.

How many women went to the tomb? Luke, likely due to his purpose in writing, gives us the most comprehensive account, but that does not mean that Mark and John are wrong nor misleading. Because Luke gives us a fuller treatment, saying that three, *and the others*, came to the tomb, does not mean that Mark is wrong, when he focuses on the three, or that John is wrong, when he only mentions Mary Magdalene.

The other seeming discrepancies are similar. If there were two angels at the tomb, then there was certainly one. Just because Mark chooses to focus on the one who spoke does not mean that another was not present. Likewise, if John and Peter ran to the tomb, then Peter certainly did. None of these inconsistencies are contradictory; they are in fact complementary – giving us a fuller picture of what actually happened that morning.

The last two seeming contradictions are also easy to explain. Mark 16:8 says that the women left the tomb and said nothing, while Luke 24:9-10 and John 20:11-18 say that the women went straight to where the disciples were staying and told them what they experienced. So which is it? It's probably both.

Let me explain. Remember Mark is telling the story through Peter's recollection. And in Luke's and John's accounts, Peter is the primary recipient of the women's message. Mark 16:8 does not mean that the women never told anyone what they had experienced. If that were the case, we wouldn't have this event recorded in three of the Gospels. No, what is clearly meant by Mark is that the women told no one other than Peter and the ten. In other words, they did not blab along the way throughout the streets of Jerusalem, but kept the information to themselves until they spoke to the disciples.

The post-resurrection encounter between Jesus and Mary Magdalene that is only recorded in John's gospel does not present a problem either. Each account contains unique elements that come from being written by unique individuals with particular perspectives. Considering these different perspectives, the level of unity and cohesion the resurrection accounts have is amazing.

Objection #2
The resurrection story developed over many centuries and was not held by the earliest Christians.

Recently, several scholars have asserted that belief in the resurrection developed over many years, as the apostles and their followers created the narrative. This revisionist account turned Jesus into a miracle-working god-man. These stories were later codified and written back into the Bible at a much later date.[1]

While this is a common claim, it simply isn't true. Many reasons exist to believe that from its earliest days the church taught the resurrection of Jesus as a key and foundational doctrine. Chief among these reasons is the early dating of some of Paul's writings.

As we have already established, after his conversion Paul experienced a 180-degree shift in his thinking and actions. He went from persecuting and killing Christians to planting churches and preaching Jesus. During this time, Paul wrote several letters to the first-century churches that he had established in Asia Minor. One of those churches was in Corinth. Paul's first letter to the Corinthians is dated at approximately AD 55, about twenty-five years after the death and resurrection of Christ. In this letter, Paul says:

> *For what I received I passed on to you as of first
> importance: that Christ died for our sins according
> to the Scriptures, that he was buried, that he was
> raised on the third day according to the Scriptures,*

---

1   Variations of this teaching have been promoted by scholars such as D. F. Strauss, Rudolf Bultmann, and more recently, Bart Ehrman.

*and that he appeared to Cephas, and then to the
Twelve. After that, he appeared to more than five
hundred of the brothers at the same time, most
of whom are still living, though some have fallen
asleep. Then he appeared to James, then to all the
apostles, and last of all he appeared to me also, as
to one abnormally born.*[1]

This is important for two reasons. First, it establishes that
the resurrection was and is a matter of necessary importance
for followers of Christ. Second, it gives us a time frame from
which to work backward by establishing an approximate date
for when Christians started believing and teaching that Jesus
had in fact risen from the dead. Many of Paul's writings are
dated as some of the earliest in the New Testament
(including 1 Corinthians) – even earlier than
the Gospel accounts themselves.

*...it is clear that the
resurrection belief
did not develop
over many years...*

First Corinthians 15 alludes to a meeting
that took place between Paul and several
prominent disciples, including Peter (Acts
9) during Paul's first trip to Jerusalem. The
book of Galatians fills in the story by telling
us that the gap between Paul's conversion and
his first trip to Jerusalem was three years (Galatians 1:18). It is
commonly held that Jesus was crucified around AD 30, and
Paul's conversion happened in approximately AD 33, meaning
that Paul's visit to Jerusalem was at most six years removed
from the actual event.

When viewed in light of Paul's letters to the Corinthians
and the Galatians, it is clear that the resurrection belief did not
develop over many years, to be inserted later into the narrative,
but was in fact a crucial part of the redemptive story from the
very beginning.

---

1   1 Corinthians 15:3-8.

Objection #3

The Gospels are not talking about a literal resurrection, but a spiritual or metaphorical resurrection.

This is a way that some have attempted to reconcile a naturalistic worldview with the Christian faith. They conclude that since the Bible is a complex and ancient book about faith, the resurrection accounts of Jesus do not need to be taken literally to be believed. When the Bible claims that Christ rose from the dead, it does not mean He actually rose from the dead but that He has risen in the hearts and the minds of His followers.

This position has numerous problems. First, we have shown that the majority of both believing and doubting scholars agree that the earliest witnesses (the disciples, James, and Paul) believed that Jesus physically rose from the dead. There is no indication whatsoever that any of the New Testament writers believed Jesus' resurrection was anything but physical and literal.

Jesus implored Mary not to touch Him (John 20:17). Jesus invited Thomas to touch the holes in His hands and His feet (John 20:24-29). He cooked for and ate with the disciples after His resurrection (John 21:9-12; Acts 1:4). Jesus appeared physically to the apostle Paul (Acts 9). Paul asserts that the physical resurrection of Christ is the basis of our hope (1 Corinthians 15). Paul even brings up the resurrection as he defends himself before King Agrippa, asserting that the resurrection is a reasonable explanation for the public and commonly known facts surrounding Christ's death (Acts 26:12-32).

While these accounts do not prove the physical resurrection, they make it clear that the first-century church believed and taught that the resurrection was not just a spiritual occurrence.

Objection #4

Jesus' body was stolen from the tomb.

The irony of this objection is that it is as old as the resurrection account itself. This is the first lie the chief priests and elders devised to undermine the reports of Jesus' resurrection.

> When the chief priests had met with the elders and devised a plan, they gave the soldiers a large sum of money, telling them, "You are to say, 'His disciples came during the night and stole him away while we were asleep.' If this report gets to the governor, we will satisfy him and keep you out of trouble." So the soldiers took the money and did as they were instructed. And this story has been widely circulated among the Jews to this very day.[1]

There are several reasons this objection does not make sense. First, just hours before the supposed body snatching, Jesus' disciples were cowering in fear of the Roman authorities. All of them except John had abandoned Jesus at the cross, fearful that they might share His fate. How likely is it that a group of untrained cowards could gain the necessary courage to carry out such a plan? Second, this would have been inappropriate Sabbath activity for Jewish men that would have aroused suspicion from the Romans and the Jews. Third, the Roman governor, Pilate, had the tomb sealed and guards placed outside to keep the disciples from stealing Jesus' body and claiming a resurrection.

...there is no hint of anyone denying they had seen the resurrected Christ.

The next day, the one after Preparation Day, the chief priests and the Pharisees went to Pilate. "Sir," they said, "we remember that while he was still alive that deceiver said, 'After three days I will rise again.' So give the order for the tomb to be made secure until the third day. Otherwise, his disciples may come

---

1   Matthew 28:12-15.

and steal the body and tell the people that he has been raised from the dead. This last deception will be worse than the first."

"Take a guard," Pilate answered. "Go, make the tomb as secure as you know how." So they went and made the tomb secure by putting a seal on the stone and posting the guard.[1]

How would this motley crew of fisherman, tax collectors, and political idealists overpower the Roman guards? How would they move the stone? If there was any evidence for the stolen body theory, why were the disciples not punished by the Romans? Where would they have taken the body? If they did steal the body, why was the resurrection so widely known that it even made its way to King Agrippa's ears? Possibly the most pressing question is this: If Jesus' body was stolen, how do we explain so many people dying for a lie?

One of our universally accepted facts is that the disciples believed Jesus died and they had post-resurrection experiences with Him. Even when facing pain, persecution, and death, none of these men or women ever recanted or wavered in their testimony. They all went to their graves believing and proclaiming that Jesus rose from the dead and that they had seen Him. If Jesus' body was stolen, what do we do with the agreed-upon facts that Paul and James converted under strange circumstances? How do we explain the apostle Paul boldly proclaiming that the resurrected Jesus had appeared to over five hundred people at one time, most of whom were still living at the time Paul wrote his letters? This kind of assertion, written to the church of Corinth in approximately AD 55, would have been easy to discount, but there is no hint of anyone denying they had seen the resurrected Christ.

---

1   Matthew 27:62-66.

Objection #5

The witnesses went to the wrong tomb.

Some have conjectured the women and disciples simply went to the wrong tomb and that is why they could not find Jesus' body. This argument is very improbable for several reasons. First, Jesus was buried in the tomb of a prominent member of the Jewish ruling council. If there was any confusion over the place where He was laid, the disciples could have simply asked Joseph which tomb was his.

Second, the women had followed Joseph and Nicodemus when the two men went to the tomb (John 19:38-42) prior to the day of preparation. They knew where they were going. They had been there before (Luke 23:55).

Third, the Romans had placed guards around the tomb, so the burial site was well known. The Jewish leaders feared the disciples would steal Jesus' body and claim that He had risen from the dead. If the women or disciples had really based their claims on the wrong tomb, the Jewish leaders would have quickly produced Jesus' body in order to silence any talk of resurrection.

Lastly, this hypothesis does not sufficiently answer the post-resurrection appearances of the Lord. If Jesus' body was simply misplaced, how do we explain the unwavering testimony of His followers that they saw Him after His death?

Other Objections

Other ideas have been circulated throughout the years to explain the events surrounding the resurrection, but each one seems more fraught with problems than the next. Here are some examples of additional objections:

Is it likely that Jesus' body was not buried but simply thrown onto a trash heap and burned?

Regardless of their personal hostility toward Him, the Jewish leaders of Jesus' day would have been bound by ritual purity to give Him a proper burial. To not do so would have damaged their credibility and authority as leaders and defenders of the Jewish traditions. Josephus says that crucified Jewish criminals were afforded funeral rites and taken down and buried before sunset. Additionally, a temple scroll from the first century discovered at Qumran specifically calls for the burial of crucified Jews.

Is it possible that Jesus really didn't die on the cross?

Volumes have been written on this topic. People did not survive crucifixion. To be crucified was to die.[1] The Romans were well trained and brutal. Even though they were ancient people, these soldiers knew when someone was dead. There is no possible way these trained killers would have taken a living person off the cross.

Did the disciples have an experience not based on reality?

This protest suggests that the disciples had an experience of shared psychosis. While this position could explain the experiences of the disciples, it appeals to something that is as miraculous as the resurrection itself. There is no psychological basis for this type of experience. For hundreds of people, in dozens of places, and at various times to experience the same hallucination is simply attempting to explain away one miracle with another.[2]

The Hope of the Resurrection

Whether we recognize it or not, we all need hope. I think this is John's greatest asset when it comes to talking with Phil. At some point in his life, Phil is going to be faced with the cold-hard

---

1   William Lane Craig, *The Son Rises: The Historical Evidence for the Resurrection of Jesus* (Eugene, OR: Wipf and Stock, 2000), 36-40.

2   Some have even asserted that Jesus was an alien. This is one of the more absurd claims made about Him by otherwise intelligent people. These kinds of appeals only underscore the unwillingness of some to believe despite the evidence.

realities of this life. In those dark and broken moments, he will begin to desire something that all humans at one point or another desire – hope. All of us long to believe death is not the end, separation from those we love is not permanent, and all that we are is not snuffed out the moment we die. Humans want to believe in the resurrection. We just need a reason to begin asking the questions.

Conclusion

Jesus died on a cross. This fact is beyond dispute. But that's not the end of the story. The resurrection isn't just the best explanation of the fact surrounding Jesus' death; it is also the best possible news for humanity. Our God has come and lived among us. He has faced sin, death, and the grave and defeated them all. And that is really good news.

Discussion Questions

- Will this chapter make a difference in how to start conversations about the resurrection? If so, how?

- What objections to the resurrection have you struggled with in the past?

- What reason for the resurrection do you find most compelling?

- What reason do you find least compelling?

- How will this chapter change the way you begin and progress through conversations about the resurrection?

About the Authors

Ryan Whitson · Dennis Moles · Darrell Dooyema · John Hopper · Danny Loe · Craig Reynolds · Doug Arendsee

Ryan Whitson

Ryan serves as campus pastor at Good News Community Church near Denver, Colorado, and as an adjunct professor of philosophy and religious studies. He has earned degrees at Westmont College (BA), Liberty University (MDiv), and Talbot School of Theology (DMin). Ryan is the author of *Dangerous Discipleship* (Parson Place Press). He loves time with his family, sports, coffee shops, and good books.

Ryan may be contacted at ryanwhitson8@gmail.com.

Dennis Moles

Dennis B. Moles is a writer, speaker, and content developer for Our Daily Bread Ministries in Grand Rapids, Michigan. Dennis is a graduate of Cedarville University, Moody Theological Seminary, Calvin Theological Seminary, and is currently finishing his doctorate at Talbot School of Theology. He is the author of *Beyond Reasonable Doubt: The Truth about the Bible*, *Beyond Reasonable Doubt: Examining the Reliability of the Bible* (Bible study), and *Being Jesus Online: Biblical Wisdom for a Wired World*. He lives with his wife and three children in Jenison, Michigan.

You can follow Dennis on twitter @DennisMoles.

Danny Loe

Danny Loe (ThM, 1999, Dallas Theological Seminary; present DMin candidate, Talbot School of Theology) has served with CRU for forty years, primarily in East Asia. He and his wife, Rebekah, now live in Budapest, Hungary. Danny teaches Bible courses throughout Eastern Europe. They are blessed with four adult children, David, Jonathan, Grace, and Susanna.

Danny may be contacted at dannydloe@gmail.com.

John Hopper

John serves as the executive pastor at BridgePoint Bible Church in Houston, Texas. He has earned degrees at Trinity University (BA), the University of Houston (MEd), Bethel Seminary (MA, transformational leadership), and Talbot School of Theology (DMin). He loves his family, most any activity that makes him sweat, and reading a good book.

To learn more about John, see *www.jkhlibrary.com.*

Douglas Arendsee

Douglas Arendsee is retired from the Civil Service as Wyoming Air National Guard chaplain technician and is currently the Air National Guard assistant to the commandant of the United States Air Force Chaplain Corps College. He graduated from the Air Force Academy in 1974 and Dallas Theological Seminary in 1986. He has done doctoral-level work at a number of institutions, most recently at Talbot Seminary. Doug and his wife, Peggy, have six married children and nine grandchildren. They recently moved to Midlothian, Texas.

Darrell Dooyema

Darrell and his wife, Annette, work with the International Student Ministry of The Navigators in Colorado Springs, Colorado. He directs a summer program in Norway, where college students from the US and other countries come to explore difficult questions of faith, gain missions experience, and grow in their walk with Jesus. Darrell also teaches philosophy in the community college system of Colorado and enjoys the chance to help students think about the ultimate questions of life. He has degrees from Wheaton College (BA), Denver Seminary (MA), and Talbot School of Theology (DMin). While he loves to ski and to surf, his greatest joy (and most exciting challenge) is his three young children, Dylan (10), Jared (6), and Eva Alice (4).

Darrell may be contacted at Ddooyema@gmail.com.

Craig Reynolds

Craig is the associate pastor and minister of education at Mount Zion Baptist Church in Alexandria, Alabama. He served as senior pastor of Cove Creek Baptist Church in Glencoe, Alabama, for twelve years. He holds a BS degree from Troy University, an MDiv from New Orleans Baptist Theological Seminary, and a DMin from Talbot School of Theology. He has been happily married to his wife, Shelby, for eighteen years and has two children, a daughter, Emma, and a son, Joseph.

Craig may be contacted at pastorcraigr@gmail.com.